Levantine Arabic Verbs

Conjugation Tables and Grammar

Matthew Aldrich

Revised edition published 2020

ISBN: 978-0998641133

website: www.lingualism.com

email: contact@lingualism.com

Contents

Introduction

Levantine Colloquial Arabic is an umbrella term for the continuum of dialects spoken in Lebanon, Syria, Palestine, Israel, and Jordan, a region collectively known as the Levant. Although there are some differences in pronunciation, vocabulary, and grammar, the varieties of Arabic spoken in this region are, to a large extent, mutually intelligible. It would be confusing and ineffective to try to include several regional varieties in the conjugation tables in this book. For this reason, one variety, Lebanese Arabic, has been chosen. Even if you plan to travel to—or just talk with speakers from—other parts of the Levant, you will be able to communicate using the Lebanese dialect and accent successfully. If your aim is to mimic a local dialect, you will only need to make minor adjustments, which you will pick up over time by listening to locals.

The concept of this book has been modeled after two other Lingualism titles: *Egyptian Colloquial Arabic Verbs* and *The Big Fat Book of Egyptian Arabic Verbs.* The former focuses on classifying verbs into patterns while the latter gives conjugation tables for the most common verbs, along with example sentences. **Levantine Arabic Verbs: Conjugation Tables and Grammar** does both, including tables of the most commonly used verbs in daily life and example sentences, as well as providing a system of verb classifications which allows you to conjugate any of the 750 verbs shown in the indexes.

The materials in this book are largely based on surveys completed by native speakers of Lebanese Arabic. I found that individuals, even those in the same city (namely, Beirut), sometimes disagree on the vowels used in some verbs. In such cases, I chose the most common, acceptable form. Keep this in mind, however, as you will hear variations among native speakers.

The conjugation tables show perfect, imperfect, bi-imperfect, imperative, and active participle forms of verbs. (These may also be known by other grammatical names, such as past, subjunctive, present, command, and present participle.) The passive participle (past participle) and verbal noun (gerund, masdar) are not included in the tables as they are used as adjectives and nouns, respectively, falling outside the scope of this book.

I want to thank Aisha El Saleous, Ibrahim Sioufi, Hoda Hilal, Mona Noureddine, and Nadine-Lama Choucaire for providing the many wonderful example sentences in this book, as well as editing and answering all of my questions to ensure a high level of accuracy and authenticity of the information. A special thanks to Nadine-Lama Choucaire for also recording the accompanying audio tracks.

How to Use This Book

Tables appear in alphabetical order, **numbered** for easy reference. In the indexes, this table is referenced as **T-62**.

Arabic verbs are traditionally grouped into **measures**. ➲ *p. 115*

The most **basic form** of an Arabic verb (the 3rd-person singular perfect tense form) is used to reference the verb, as the infinitve is in English.

A single, common **translation** of each verb is given at the top of the table. Other possible translations and meanings can be found in the example sentences and indexes.

The **persons** appear in the left column, written only in phonemic transcription so as not to distract from the verb written in Arabic. ➲ *p. 105*

Tenses and moods head each column. Study the grammar section for the usage of each. ➲ *p. 107-115*

Notes highlight idiosyncrasies of certain verbs.

Conjugated verbs appear both in Arabic script and **phonemic transcription**. ➲ *p. v-viii*

Audio tracks with the conjugated forms and example sentences for all tables are available to download for free at **www.lingualism.com/lav**

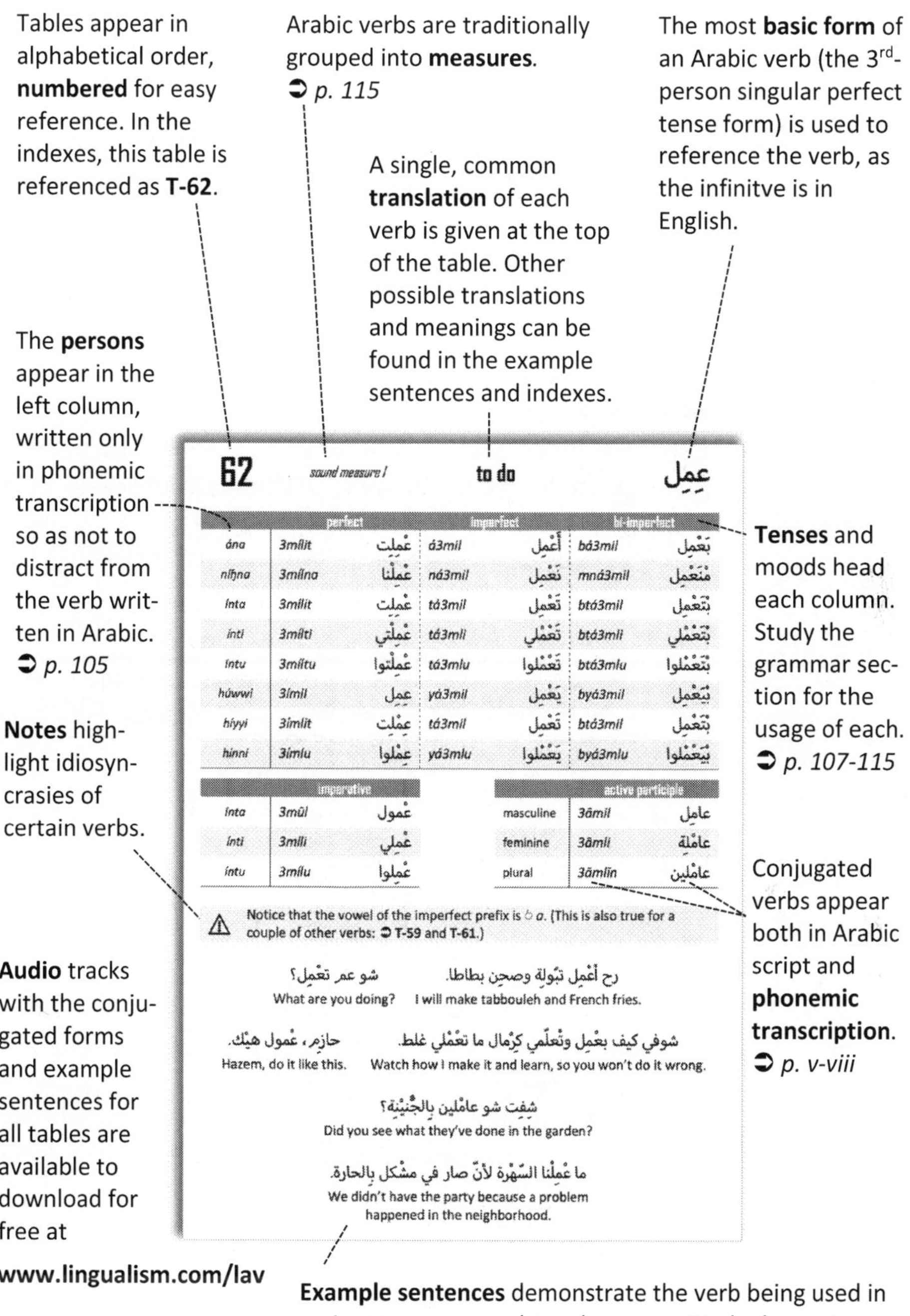

62 *sound measure I* **to do** عِمِل

	perfect		imperfect		bi-imperfect	
ána	*3mílit*	عْمِلِت	*á3mil*	أَعْمِل	*bá3mil*	بَعْمِل
níḥna	*3mílna*	عْمِلْنا	*ná3mil*	نَعْمِل	*mná3mil*	مْنَعْمِل
ínta	*3mílit*	عْمِلِت	*tá3mil*	تَعْمِل	*btá3mil*	بْتَعْمِل
ínti	*3mílti*	عْمِلْتي	*tá3mli*	تَعْمْلي	*btá3mli*	بْتَعْمْلي
íntu	*3míltu*	عْمِلْتوا	*tá3mlu*	تَعْمْلوا	*btá3mlu*	بْتَعْمْلوا
húwwi	*3ímil*	عِمِل	*yá3mil*	يَعْمِل	*byá3mil*	بْيَعْمِل
híyyi	*3ímlit*	عِمْلِت	*tá3mil*	تَعْمِل	*btá3mil*	بْتَعْمِل
hínni	*3ímlu*	عِمْلوا	*yá3mlu*	يَعْمْلوا	*byá3mlu*	بْيَعْمْلوا

	imperative	
ínta	*3mûl*	عْمول
ínti	*3míli*	عْمِلي
íntu	*3mílu*	عْمِلوا

	active participle	
masculine	*3āmil*	عامِل
feminine	*3āmli*	عامْلة
plural	*3āmlīn*	عامْلين

⚠ Notice that the vowel of the imperfect prefix is ـَ *a*. (This is also true for a couple of other verbs: ➲ T-59 and T-61.)

شو عم تعْمِل؟
What are you doing?

رح أعْمِل تبّولة وصحِن بطاطا.
I will make tabbouleh and French fries.

حازم، عْمول هيْك.
Hazem, do it like this.

شوفي كيف بعْمِل وتْعلّمي كِرْمال ما تعْمْلي غلط.
Watch how I make it and learn, so you won't do it wrong.

شِفِت شو عامْلين بِالجْنيْنة؟
Did you see what they've done in the garden?

ما عْمِلْنا السّهْرة لأنّ صار في مشْكل بِالحارة.
We didn't have the party because a problem happened in the neighborhood.

Example sentences demonstrate the verb being used in various tenses, moods, and persons. Study the sentences to better understand the range of meanings (and translations) and idiomatic usage of the verb.

Use the **Index by Table Pattern** to conjugate hundreds more common Levantine verbs.

First, find the verb you would like to conjugate in the Arabic Index (➲ *p. 133*) or English Index (➲ *p. 144*). Next to it, you will see an alphanumeric label. For example, if you look up سبح or *swim,* you will see 1s1 following the verb.

Now, go to the Index by Table Pattern (➲ *p. 118*) and find group 1s1. (Notice that 1s1 is shorthand for sound measure I, first subgroup. ➲ *p. 115-117*).

You can see سبح *swim* listed alphabetically in group 1s1. There is no conjugation table for this particular verb, but all of the verbs belonging to group 1s1 share the same conjugation pattern. Use any of the verbs that do have a table (marked **T-**) to model the conjugation of سبح.

You can, for example, look up **T-32** (table 32 on *p. 32* for the verb دفع *pay*) and substitute the three radicals (consonants) of this verb with those of سبح *swim.* If you want to say *they swim,* find the equivalent of *they pay* in table 32 (the bi-imperfect *hínni* form): بْيِدْفَعوا *biyídfa3u* and transform it into بْيِسْبَحوا *byísbaħu.*

1s1	*sound measure I* ①	
	بحش	dig
	بخع	humiliate
	بعت	send; mail
	بلع	swallow
	تبع	follow
	جرح	wound, injure, hurt
	جمع	add, add up; harvest
	حصل	obtain على
	خدع	deceive
	خلع	snatch
	دعس	step
	دعس	tread on على
T-32	دفع	pay
T-33	دقر	touch
	دهن	paint
	رفع	raise
	زحط	slip
	زرع	plant (a seed), grow (a plant)
	زعب	kick; speak harshly
T-42	سأل	ask
	سبح	swim
	سحب	withdraw
	سمح	allow, permit
	شحد	beg (for money)
	شرح	explain
	شلح	undress; take off, remove
	صنع	manufacture
	ضهر	leave; go out
	طبع	print
	طحن	grind
	طرح	subtract
	ظهر	appear
T-66	فتح	open
	فحص	examine
	فقس	click on على
	فلح	plow (field); work hard
T-71	قبض	earn
	قنع	convince

Pronunciation

Levantine Colloquial Arabic (LCA) is a spoken dialect with no official status or rules of orthography. Native speakers tend to borrow spelling conventions from Modern Standard Arabic with some accommodations to account for LCA pronunciation. Arabic script, however, is ill-suited to show the actual pronunciation of LCA, including word stress and sound changes that occur when verbs are conjugated. Even if you are comfortable with Arabic script, it is advised that you pay close attention to the phonemic transcription (and audio tracks) to determine a more precise pronunciation of verbs. IPA (International Phonetic Alphabet) symbols are found in [square brackets] in the descriptions below. You may find exceptions to the following rules, especially when it comes to words borrowed from other languages.

Consonants

The following sounds are also found in English and should pose no difficulties:

			<u>*examples*</u>
b	ب	[b] as in **b**ed	*bána* بنى *(build)*
d	د	[d̪] as in **d**og, but with the tongue touching the back of the upper teeth	*dáris* درِس *(study)*
f	ف	[f] as in **f**our	*fātūra* فاتورة *(bill)*
j	ج	[ʒ] as in plea**s**ure and bei**ge**	*jísim* جِسِم *(body)*
h	ه	[h] as in **h**ouse	*hājam* هاجم *(attack)*
k	ك	[k] as in **k**id	*ákal* اكل *(eat)*
l	ل	[l] a light ***l*** as in **l**ove	*líbis* لِبِس *(get dressed)*
m	م	[m] as in **m**oon	*māt* مات *(die)*
n	ن	[n] as in **n**ice	*nísi* نِسي *(forget)*
p	ب	[p] appears in some foreign borrowings	*spōr* سْبور *(sport)*
s	س ث	[s] as in **s**un	*síni* سِنة *(year)*
š	ش	[ʃ] as in **sh**ow	*šū* شو *(what)*
t	ت	[t̪] as in **t**ie, but with the tongue touching the back of the upper teeth	*tlāti* تلاتِة *(three)*
v	ف	[v] appears in some foreign borrowings	*mūvī* موفي *(movie)*
w	و	[w] as in **w**ord	*wēn* وين *(where)*
y	ي	[j] as in **y**es	*yíktub* يِكْتُب *(he writes)*
z	ز ذ	[z] as in **z**oo	*zār* زار *(visit)*

The following sounds have no equivalent in English and require special attention. However, some exist in other languages you may be familiar with.

r	ر	[ɾ] tapped (flapped) as in the Spanish ca**r**a, or the Scottish pronunciation of t**r**ee	*ráma* رمى *(throw)*
ɣ	غ	[ɣ] very similar to a guttural ***r*** as in the French Pa**r**is, or the German **r**ot	*ɣēr* غيْر *(different)*
x	خ	[x] as in the German do**ch**, Spanish ro**j**o, or Scottish lo**ch**	*áxad* اخد *(take)*
q	ق	[q] like ***k*** but further back, almost in the throat, with the tongue touching the uvula	*qanāt* قناة *(channel)*
ɧ	ح	[ħ] like a strong, breathy ***h***, as if you were trying to fog up a window	*yíɧfur* يِحْفُر *(he digs)*
3	ع	[ʕ] a voiced glottal stop, as if you had opened your mouth under water and constricted your throat to prevent choking and then released the constriction with a sigh	*3írif* عِرِف *(know)*
ʔ	ء ق	[ʔ] an unvoiced glottal stop, as [ʕ] above, but with a wispy, unvoiced sigh; or more simply put, like the constriction separating the vowels in uh-oh	*ʔíbil* قِبِل *(accept)*

The following sounds also have no equivalent in English but are emphatic versions of otherwise familiar sounds. An emphatic consonant is produced by pulling the tongue back toward the pharynx (throat), spreading the sides of the tongue wide as if you wanted to bite down on both sides of your tongue, and producing a good puff of air from the lungs.

ḍ	ض	[dˤ] emphatic ***d***	*ḍárab* ضرب *(hit)*
ṣ	ص	[sˤ] emphatic ***s***	*ṣúbuɧ* صُبُح *(morning)*
ṭ	ط	[tˤ] emphatic ***t***	*ṭálab* طلب *(ask)*
ẓ	ظ	[zˤ] emphatic ***z***	*būẓa* بوظة *(ice cream)*

Vowels

In LCA, vowels have some fluidity to their quality—their pronunciation is affected by neighboring consonants. The phonemic transcription offers an approximation based on the Arabic script. However, you should rely on the audio tracks to mimic a more precise pronunciation. Foreign words, in particular, may deviate from the rules below. Final vowels may be marked as long, but in reality, are often pronounced somewhat shorter.

			examples
a	ـَ	The most versatile of the vowels, **a** may be pronounced a number of ways, most commonly [æ] as in c**a**t (but with the jaw not quite as lowered as in English); sometimes [ɛ] as in b**e**d, but sometimes more open, as the French é [e]; [a] as in st**o**ck when in the same syllable with ***ɧ*** or ***3***; usually [ɑ] as in f**a**ther (but shorter) when in the same word as ***q, ɖ, ʂ, ʈ, ʐ,*** or, in most cases, ***r***	*kátab* كَتَب *(write)* *ɧaʈʈ* حَطّ *(put)* *ma3* مَع *(with)* *ɖárab* ضَرَب *(hit)* *áʂɣar* أَصْغَر *(younger)*
ā	ـا	[æ:] / [a:] / [ɑ:] as with ***a*** above but longer	*nām* نام *(sleep)* *jā3* جاع *(get hungry)* *maqāl* مقال *(article)*
ã	ـان ـون	[ɑ̃] (nasal) as in the French écr**an**	*ēkrã* ايْكْرون *(sunscreen)*
e	ـٚـ	[ɛ] as in b**e**d, found in some foreign words.	*esprésso* اسْبْرِسّو *(espresso)*
ē	ـيْـا	[e:] as in pl**ay** (but without the glide to [j])	*wēn* ويْن *(where)* *kētib* كاتِب *(writer)*
i	ـِ	[ɪ] as in k**i**d; [ɛ] as in b**e**d when in the same syllable with ***ɧ*** or ***3***; when in the same word as ***q, ɖ, ʂ, ʈ,*** or ***ʐ,*** [ɨ] with the tongue pulled back a bit	*3ílim* عِلِم *(science)* *šíliɧ* شِلِح *(undress)* *ɖidd* ضِدّ *(against)*
ī	ـي	[i:] as in sk**i**; [ɛ:] and [ɨ:] as with **i** above (but longer)	*fī* في *(there is)* *ybī3* يْبيع *(he sells)* *-ʂʂīn* الصّين *(China*
o	ـٗ	[o] as in kn**ow** (but shorter and without the glide to [w])	*doktōr* دُكْتوْر *(doctor)*
ō	ـوْ	[o:] as with **o** above but longer	*nōm* نوْم *(sleep)*
õ	ـون	[ɔ̃] (nasal) as in the French marr**on**	*pãnʈalõ* بنْطَلون *(pants)*
u	ـُ	[ʊ] as in b**oo**k	*yíʈlub* يِطْلُب *(he orders)*
ū	ـُو	[u:] as in m**oo**n	*šū* شو *(what)*

Also to Note:

- The pronunciation rules laid out above are guidelines, rules of thumb. There are in fact many exceptions to these simplified pronunciation rules. Sound changes occur in many instances, according to grammatical inflections such as verb conjugation. A treatment of these, pertaining to grammar, lies outside the scope of this book. Look for patterns in the example sentences to come up with your own rules, and, of course, ask a native speaker when in doubt.
- ـة is usually pronounced *-i*, but is pronounced *-a* following certain consonants. Keep this in mind when using a table to model the conjugation of a different verb.
- Attempts have been made to maintain a consistent orthography (spelling) in the Arabic script throughout this book. You will, of course, see various spellings of words by native speakers, as there are no official spelling rules for dialects. *Tashkeel* (diacritic marks) are not normally used by Arabs in their writing but are used in this book for the benefit of learners. Full tashkeel is given in the tables, while a slightly more minimalist approach is taken in the example sentences. To avoid clutter and make the text more readable, fatha is assumed to be the default vowel and is not normally written. Also, some very common words and affixes are written without tashkeel:

ـية	*-íyyi*
الـ	*il- / l-, li-* (followed by shadda when assimilated before certain consonants ("sun letters").
اللي	*ílli*
و	*u, w*

Accompanying audio available at:

www.lingualism.com/lav

1 *irregular defective measure I* **to come** إجا

	perfect		imperfect		bi-imperfect	
ána	*jīt*	جيت	*íji*	إجي	*bíji*	بِجي
níħna	*jīna*	جينا	*níji*	نِجي	*mníji*	مْنِجي
ínta	*jīt*	جيت	*tíji*	تِجي	*btíji*	بْتِجي
ínti	*jīti*	جيتي	*tíji*	تِجي	*btíji*	بْتِجي
íntu	*jītu*	جيتوا	*tíju*	تِجوا	*btíju*	بْتِجوا
húwwi	*íja*	إجا	*yíji*	يِجي	*byíji*	بْيِجي
híyyi	*íjit*	إجِت	*tíji*	تِجي	*btíji*	بْتِجي
hínni	*íju*	إجوا	*yíju*	يِجوا	*byíju*	بْيِجوا

	imperative	
ínta	*tá3a*	تَعا
ínti	*tá3i*	تَعي
íntu	*tá3u*	تَعوا

	active participle	
masculine	*jēy*	جاي
feminine	*jēyi*	جايِة
plural	*jēyīn*	جايين

① Only the third-person perfect forms begin with إ *i-*.
② The positive imperative is completely unrelated to the verb.
③ The masculine active participle is also commonly pronounced جايي *jēyi*.

جيت لعِنْدك ودقّيْت الباب، ما حدا فتح.
I came to your house and knocked on the door, but no one answered.

لمّا تِجي مِن السّوق دِقّيلي.
When you get back from shopping, call me.

بْتِجي لعِنْدي الشّغالِة مرّة بالْشّهر.
The cleaning lady comes to my house once a month.

أيمْتى جايين؟
When are you are coming?

تعوا عَ بُكْرا الصُّبْح، مْنِفْطر سَوا.
Come tomorrow morning and we'll have breakfast together.

2 *irregular measure I* **to take** أَخَد

	perfect		imperfect		bi-imperfect	
ána	*ʔaxádit*	أَخَدِت	*ʔēxud*	آخُد	*bēxud*	باخُد
níħna	*ʔaxádna*	أَخَدْنا	*nēxud*	ناخُد	*mnēxud*	مْناخُد
ínta	*ʔaxádit*	أَخَدِت	*tēxud*	تاخُد	*btēxud*	بْتاخُد
ínti	*ʔaxádti*	أَخَدْتي	*tēxdi*	تاخْدي	*btēxdi*	بْتاخْدي
íntu	*ʔaxádtu*	أَخَدْتوا	*tēxdu*	تاخْدوا	*btēxdu*	بْتاخْدوا
húwwi	*ʔáxad*	أَخَد	*yēxud*	ياخُد	*byēxud*	بْياخُد
híyyi	*ʔáxadit*	أَخَدِت	*tēxud*	تاخُد	*btēxud*	بْتاخُد
hínni	*ʔáxadu*	أَخَدوا	*yēxdu*	ياخْدوا	*byēxdu*	بْياخْدوا

	imperative	
ínta	*xud*	خُد
ínti	*xídi*	خِدي
íntu	*xídu*	خِدوا

	active participle	
masculine	*ʔēxid (mēxid)*	آخِد (ماخِد)
feminine	*ʔēxdi (mēxdi)*	آخْدِة (ماخْدِة)
plural	*ʔēxdīn (mēxdīn)*	آخْدين (ماخْدين)

① The imperfect forms have a long vowel, unlike regular measure I verbs.
② The active participle has a less common variant beginning with مـ *m-*.
③ أكل *ʔákal* (**T-4**) is the twin of this irregular verb.

أخدِت علْبِة مناكير مِن الخْزانِة.
I took the nail polish box out of the closet.

خِدوا خيكُن الصْغير عالمدْرسِة معْكُن.
Take your little brother with you to school.

ما بْتاخُد ولا شي بْدون إذِن.
Don't take anything without permission.

كان آخِد معو عِدِّة صيْد.
He has taken a fishing kit with him.

خِدي حْمِلي معي الغْراض.
Help me carry these bags.

3 *sound measure IV* **to announce** أَعْلَن

	perfect		imperfect		bi-imperfect	
ána	ʔa3lánit	أَعْلَنِت	í3lun	إعْلُن	bí3lun	بِعْلُن
níḫna	ʔa3lánna	أَعْلَنّا	ní3lun	نِعْلُن	mní3lun	مْنِعْلُن
ínta	ʔa3lánit	أَعْلَنِت	tí3lun	تِعْلُن	btí3lun	بْتِعْلُن
ínti	ʔa3lánti	أَعْلَنْتي	ti3ílni	تِعِلْني	bti3ílni	بْتِعِلْني
íntu	ʔa3lántu	أَعْلَنْتوا	ti3ílnu	تِعِلْنوا	bti3ílnu	بْتِعِلْنوا
húwwi	ʔá3lan	أَعْلَن	yí3lun	يِعْلُن	byí3lun	بْيِعْلُن
híyyi	ʔá3lanit	أَعْلَنِت	tí3lun	تِعْلُن	btí3lun	بْتِعْلُن
hínni	ʔá3lanu	أَعْلَنوا	yi3ílnu	يِعِلْنوا	byi3ílnu	بْيِعِلْنوا

	imperative	
ínta	3lūn	عْلون
ínti	3líni	عْلِني
íntu	3línu	عْلِنوا

	active participle	
masculine	mú3lin	مُعْلِن
feminine	mú3lini	مُعْلِنِة
plural	mu3linīn	مُعْلِنين

الدّوْلِة أعْلنِت اليوْم عِطْلِة رسْمية.

The government has declared today an official holiday.

عْلون بدّك دمّ مِنْشان عملية القلْب المفْتوح لبيّك.

Spread the word that you need blood for your father's open-heart surgery.

ما حتِعِلْني عنْدِك صالوْن تجْميل؟

Won't you advertise that you have a beauty parlor?

رح نِعْلُن الإضْراب يوْم التّنينْ.

We declare the strike [will be] on Monday.

أنا ويارا أعْلنّا عِرِسْنا الشّهْر الجّاي.

Yara and I announced that our wedding ceremony will be next month.

4 *irregular measure I* **to eat** أَكَل

	perfect		imperfect		bi-imperfect	
ána	ʔakálit	أَكَلِت	ʔēkul	آكُل	bēkul	باكُل
níḫna	ʔakálna	أَكَلْنا	nēkul	ناكُل	mnēkul	مْناكُل
ínta	ʔakálit	أَكَلِت	tēkul	تاكُل	btēkul	بْتاكُل
ínti	ʔakálti	أَكَلْتي	tēkli	تاكْلي	btēkli	بْتاكْلي
íntu	ʔakáltu	أَكَلْتوا	tēklu	تاكْلوا	btēklu	بْتاكْلوا
húwwi	ʔákal	أَكَل	yēkul	ياكُل	byēkul	بْياكُل
híyyi	ʔákalit	أَكَلِت	tēkul	تاكُل	btēkul	بْتاكُل
hínni	ʔákalu	أَكَلوا	yēklu	ياكْلوا	byēklu	بْياكْلوا

	imperative	
ínta	kul	كُل
ínti	kíli	كِلي
íntu	kílu	كِلوا

	active participle	
masculine	ʔēkil (mēkil)	آكِل (ماكِل)
feminine	ʔēkli (mēkli)	آكْلِة (ماكْلِة)
plural	ʔēklīn (mēklīn)	آكْلين (ماكْلين)

① The imperfect forms have a long vowel, unlike regular measure I verbs.
② The active participle has a less common variant beginning with مـ m-.
③ أخد ʔáxad (**T-2**) is the twin of this irregular verb.

شو جاي عَ بالْكُن تاكْلوا؟
What would you like to eat?

أكلْنا مناقيش زعْتر.
We ate thyme manakeesh.

عم باكُل كِبِّة لِبْنانية حدّا بطاطا وتبولِة.
I'm eating Lebanese kebeh with French fries and tabouleh.

آكِل جِبْنِة حلوم مِن عِنْد ألْبان جابِر جابِر بْشتورة.
He has eaten haloum cheese from Jaber Jaber Dairy in Chtaura.

كِلي معْنا.
Eat with us.

to order أَمَر

	perfect		imperfect		bi-imperfect	
ána	ʔamárit	أَمَرِت	úʔmur	أُؤْمُر	búʔmur	بُؤْمُر
níħna	ʔamárna	أَمَرْنا	núʔmur	نُؤْمُر	mnúʔmur	مْنُؤْمُر
ínta	ʔamárit	أَمَرِت	túʔmur	تُؤْمُر	btúʔmur	بْتُؤْمُر
ínti	ʔamárti	أَمَرْتي	túʔmri	تُؤْمْري	btúʔmri	بْتُؤْمْري
íntu	ʔamártu	أَمَرْتوا	túʔmru	تُؤْمْروا	btúʔmru	بْتُؤْمْروا
húwwi	ʔámar	أَمَر	yúʔmur	يُؤْمُر	byúʔmur	بْيُؤْمُر
híyyi	ʔámarit	أَمَرِت	túʔmur	تُؤْمُر	btúʔmur	بْتُؤْمُر
hínni	ʔámaru	أَمَروا	yúʔmru	يُؤْمْروا	byúʔmru	بْيُؤْمْروا

	imperative	
ínta	ʔmūr	أْمور
ínti	ʔmúri	أْمُري
íntu	3múru	أْمُروا

	active participle	
masculine	ʔēmir	آمِر
feminine	ʔēmra	آمْرَة
plural	ʔēmrīn	آمْرين

دُكْتورة عفاف أمرِت طلّابا يْخلْصوا كِتابِة أطْروحتْن هالأُسْبوع.

Dr. Afaf ordered her students to finish writing their thesis this week.

المُدير إلْياس عم يُؤْمُر لمَوَظّفين يْخلْصوا التّقارير بْسِرْعة.

The manager Elias is ordering his staff to finish the reports quickly.

مساء الخيرْ مدام، شو بْتُؤْمْري؟

Good afternoon, ma'am. Can I help you?

بْتُؤْمُر سيدي، بْتِطْلُب شي بعْد؟

Yes, sir. And would you like to order anything else?

أْمُري ماما بْجِبْلِك شي بْطريقي؟

Do you want me to bring you anything, mom?

6 *hollow measure I* **to sell** باع

	perfect		imperfect		bi-imperfect	
ána	*bí3it*	بِعِت	*bī3*	بيع	*bbī3*	بْبيع
níђna	*bí3na*	بِعْنا	*nbī3*	نْبيع	*minbī3*	مِنْبيع
ínta	*bí3it*	بِعِت	*tbī3*	تْبيع	*bitbī3*	بِتْبيع
ínti	*bí3ti*	بِعْتي	*tbī3i*	تْبيعي	*bitbī3i*	بِتْبيعي
íntu	*bí3tu*	بِعْتوا	*tbī3u*	تْبيعوا	*bitbī3u*	بِتْبيعوا
húwwi	*bē3*	باع	*ybī3*	يْبيع	*bibī3*	بيبيع
híyyi	*bē3it*	باعِت	*tbī3*	تْبيع	*bitbī3*	بِتْبيع
hínni	*bē3u*	باعوا	*ybī3u*	يْبيعوا	*bibī3u*	بيبيعوا

	imperative	
ínta	*bī3*	بيع
ínti	*bī3i*	بيعي
íntu	*bī3u*	بيعوا

	active participle	
masculine	*bēyi3*	بايِع
feminine	*bēy3a*	بايْعَة
plural	*bēy3īn*	بايْعين

باعِت كِلّ غْراض البيْت لَتْسافِر.

She sold everything in her house in order to travel.

بِسبب الإِضْراب، ما بايْعين شي اليوْم.

Because of the strike, we haven't sold anything today.

روح بيع الزّبايِن.

Go serve your customers.

بْحِبّ بيع مشْروبات بِالمهْرجانات.

I like to sell beverages at festivals.

بِتْبيع عجين كِرْمال أعْمِل مناقيش بِالبيْت؟

Do you sell dough, so that I can make pastries at home?

sound measure I

to turn

بَرَم

	perfect		imperfect		bi-imperfect	
ána	*barámit*	بَرَمِت	*íbrum*	إِبْرُم	*bíbrum*	بِبْرُم
níђna	*barámna*	بَرَمْنا	*níbrum*	نِبْرُم	*mníbrum*	مْنِبْرُم
ínta	*barámit*	بَرَمِت	*tíbrum*	تِبْرُم	*btíbrum*	بْتِبْرُم
ínti	*barámti*	بَرَمْتي	*tíbrmi*	تِبْرْمي	*btíbrmi*	بْتِبْرْمي
íntu	*barámtu*	بَرَمْتوا	*tíbrmu*	تِبْرْموا	*btíbrmu*	بْتِبْرْموا
húwwi	*báram*	بَرَم	*yíbrum*	يِبْرُم	*byíbrum*	بْيِبْرُم
híyyi	*báramit*	بَرَمِت	*tíbrum*	تِبْرُم	*btíbrum*	بْتِبْرُم
hínni	*báramu*	بَرَموا	*yíbrmu*	يِبْرْموا	*byíbrmu*	بْيِبْرْموا

	imperative	
ínta	*brūm*	بْروم
ínti	*brími*	بْرِمي
íntu	*brímu*	بْرِموا

	active participle	
masculine	*bērim*	بارِم
feminine	*bērmi*	بارْمِة
plural	*bērmīn*	بارْمين

برم الدّكاكين كِلّا وما لقى خِبِز.

He searched all the shops and didn't find bread.

العَيْلِة راحوا يِبرْموا بْجْبيْل.

The family went to visit Byblos [Jubeil].

لمى، تعي اليوْم لعِنْدي ومِنروح مْنِبْرُم بِالسّوق.

Lama, come over today, and we will go shopping.

لَوْ بْتِبرْموا لِبْنان كِلّو، ما بِتْلاقوا أطْيَب مِن الحِلْويات الطْرابِلْسية.

Even if you roam all over Lebanon, you won't find tastier sweets than those of Tripoli.

حاجِة تِبرْم المَوْضوع، هات مِن الآخِر!

Stop beating around the bush and get to the point.

8 *defective measure I* to become بقي

	perfect		imperfect		bi-imperfect	
ána	*bʔīt*	بْقيت	*íbʔa*	إِبْقى	*bíbʔa*	بِبْقى
níḫna	*bʔīna*	بْقينا	*níbʔa*	نِبْقى	*mníbʔa*	مْنِبْقى
ínta	*bʔīt*	بْقيت	*tíbʔa*	تِبْقى	*btíbʔa*	بْتِبْقى
ínti	*bʔīti*	بْقيتي	*tíbʔi*	تِبْقي	*btíbʔi*	بْتِبْقي
íntu	*bʔītu*	بْقيتوا	*tíbʔu*	تِبْقوا	*btíbʔu*	بْتِبْقوا
húwwi	*bíʔi*	بِقي	*yíbʔa*	يِبْقى	*byíbʔa*	بْيِبْقى
híyyi	*bíʔyit*	بِقْيِت	*tíbʔa*	تِبْقى	*btíbʔa*	بْتِبْقى
hínni	*bíʔyu*	بِقْيوا	*yíbʔu*	يِبْقوا	*byíbʔu*	بْيِبْقوا

	imperative	
ínta	*bʔī*	بْقي
ínti	*bʔī*	بْقي
íntu	*bʔū*	بْقوا

	active participle	
masculine	*bēʔi*	باقي
feminine	*bēʔyi*	باقْيِة
plural	*bēʔyīn*	باقْيين

بْقينا عِنْد دار عمّي للصُّبُح.

We stayed at our uncle's place until morning.

ما تِبْقي تِنْسي تْجيبيلي خِضْرة بْطريقِك وإنْتي راجْعة عالبيْت.

Don't forget to bring me vegetables on your way back home.

بْقوا على تَواصُل مع خالتِكُن سلْمى.

Stay in touch with your aunt Salma.

بِبْقى كْتير هادي وَقِت يْصير في مِشْكْلِة.

I remain very quiet when a problem arises.

بْيِبْقى تحْت الدّوش كْتير وَقِت.

He stays in the shower a long time.

9 *sound measure II* **to begin** بَلَّش

	perfect		imperfect		bi-imperfect	
ána	ballášit	بَلَّشِت	bálliš	بَلِّش	bbálliš	بْبَلِّش
níђna	ballášna	بَلَّشْنا	nbálliš	نْبَلِّش	minbálliš	مِنبَلِّش
ínta	ballášit	بَلَّشِت	tbálliš	تْبَلِّش	bitbálliš	بِتْبَلِّش
ínti	ballášti	بَلَّشْتي	tbállši	تْبَلْشي	bitbállši	بِتْبَلْشي
íntu	balláštu	بَلَّشْتوا	tbállšu	تْبَلْشوا	bitbállšu	بِتْبَلْشوا
húwwi	bállaš	بَلَّش	ybálliš	يْبَلِّش	bibálliš	بيبَلِّش
híyyi	bállašit	بَلَّشِت	tbálliš	تْبَلِّش	bitbálliš	بِتْبَلِّش
hínni	bállašu	بَلَّشوا	ybállšu	يْبَلْشوا	bibállšu	بيبَلْشوا

	imperative	
ínta	bálliš	بَلِّش
ínti	bállši	بَلْشي
íntu	bállšu	بَلْشوا

	active participle	
masculine	mbálliš	مْبَلِّش
feminine	mbálliši	مْبَلْشِة
plural	mballšīn	مْبَلْشين

بلّشوا عرْض الفيلْم.

They started showing the movie.

رح تْبلِّش سهْرِتا عالتّمانِة.

Her party will start at 8.

ما تْبلْشوا رقْص مِن دوني.

Don’t begin dancing without me.

شْتـري الخِضْرة مِنْشان بلِّش جهِّز الفتّوش.

Buy the vegetables so that I can start preparing fattoush.

بِتْبلِّش الأخْبار عالتّمانِة الْمسا.

The news starts at eight in the evening.

مْبلْشين شِغِل بكّير.

They began work early.

10 *sound measure I* to leave تَرَك

	perfect		imperfect		bi-imperfect	
ána	*tarákit*	تَركِت	*ítruk*	إتْرُك	*bítruk*	بِترُك
níḫna	*tarákna*	تَركْنا	*nítruk*	نِترُك	*mnítruk*	مْنِترُك
ínta	*tarákit*	تَركِت	*títruk*	تِترُك	*btítruk*	بْتِترُك
ínti	*tarákti*	تَركْتي	*títrki*	تِترْكي	*btítrki*	بْتِترْكي
íntu	*taráktu*	تَركْتوا	*títrku*	تِترْكوا	*btítrku*	بْتِترْكوا
húwwi	*tárak*	تَرَك	*yítruk*	يِترُك	*byítruk*	بْيِترُك
híyyi	*tárakit*	تَركِت	*títruk*	تِترُك	*btítruk*	بْتِترُك
hínni	*táraku*	تَركوا	*yítrku*	يِترْكوا	*byítrku*	بْيِترْكوا

	imperative	
ínta	*trūk*	تْروك
ínti	*tríki*	تْرِكي
íntu	*tríku*	تْرِكوا

	active participle	
masculine	*tērik*	تارِك
feminine	*tērki*	تارْكِة
plural	*tērkīn*	تارْكين

⚠ Adding pronoun object suffixes can affect a verb's form and pronunciation. In the second example below, تْروك *trūk* becomes *trík-ni.*

دَرَس فْرَنْسي لكم شهِر وبعْديْن ترك.

He studied French for a few months, and then he stopped.

تْرِكْني لَوَحْدي. بدّي أعْرِف إدْرُس.

Leave me alone. I'm trying to study.

مُراد بْيِترُك الضَّيْعة كِلّ سِنِة.

Mourad leaves the village every year.

ما بِترُك الأَوْلاد لَوَحْدُن يِلْعبوا بِالطّريق.

I don't let the children play alone in the street.

تْرِكي الدِّخّان، أحْسن لصحّتك.

Stop smoking. It's better for your health.

to treat تْعامَل

	perfect		imperfect		bi-imperfect	
ána	*t3āmálit*	تْعامَلت	*it3āmal*	إتْعامَل	*bit3āmal*	بِتْعامَل
níḫna	*t3āmálna*	تْعامَلْنا	*nit3āmal*	نِتْعامَل	*mnit3āmal*	مْنِتْعامَل
ínta	*t3āmálit*	تْعامَلت	*tit3āmal*	تِتْعامَل	*btit3āmal*	بْتِتْعامَل
ínti	*t3āmálti*	تْعامَلْتي	*tit3āmali*	تِتْعاملي	*btit3āmali*	بْتِتْعاملي
íntu	*t3āmáltu*	تْعامَلْتوا	*tit3āmalu*	تِتْعاملوا	*btit3āmalu*	بْتِتْعاملوا
húwwi	*t3āmal*	تْعامَل	*yit3āmal*	يِتْعامَل	*byit3āmal*	بْيِتْعامَل
híyyi	*t3āmalit*	تْعامَلِت	*tit3āmal*	تِتْعامَل	*btit3āmal*	بْتِتْعامَل
hínni	*t3āmalu*	تْعامَلوا	*yit3āmalu*	يِتْعاملوا	*byit3āmalu*	بْيِتْعاملوا

	imperative	
ínta	*t3āmal*	تْعامَل
ínti	*t3āmali*	تْعامَلي
íntu	*t3āmalu*	تْعامَلوا

	active participle	
masculine	*mit3āmal*	مِتْعامَل
feminine	*mit3āmali*	مِتْعامَلِة
plural	*mit3āmalīn*	مِتْعامَلين

سلْمى تْعاملِت مع طْلّابا بِالصّفّ عن طريق ألْعاب تعْليمية.

Salma worked with her students in class using educational games.

عم إتْعامل مع شِرْكِة تِجارية لعبّي الدِّكّانِة.

I'm dealing with a trading company in order to fill my shop.

عبد وزيْنب بْتِتْعاملوا مع بعْض لتْخلّصو المشْروع.

Abed and Zainab, work together to finish the project.

ما تْعاملوا بعْض بْوَحْشنه.

Don't treat each other harshly.

مِتْعامْلِة مع مكْتب التّوْظيف هَيْدا مرْتين.

I have dealt with his employment agency twice.

12 *sound measure V* **to learn** تْعَلَّم

	perfect		imperfect		bi-imperfect	
ána	*t3allámit*	تْعلَّمِت	*it3állam*	إتْعَلَّم	*bit3állam*	بِتْعَلَّم
níḫna	*t3allámna*	تْعلَّمْنا	*nit3állam*	نِتْعَلَّم	*mnit3állam*	مْنِتْعَلَّم
ínta	*t3allámit*	تْعلَّمِت	*tit3állam*	تِتْعَلَّم	*btit3állam*	بْتِتْعَلَّم
ínti	*t3allámti*	تْعَلَّمْتي	*tit3állami*	تِتْعَلَّمي	*btit3állami*	بْتِتْعَلَّمي
íntu	*t3allámtu*	تْعلَّمْتوا	*tit3államu*	تِتْعَلَّموا	*btit3államu*	بْتِتْعَلَّموا
húwwi	*t3állam*	تْعلَّم	*yit3állam*	يِتْعَلَّم	*byit3állam*	بْيِتْعَلَّم
híyyi	*t3államit*	تْعلَّمِت	*tit3állam*	تِتْعَلَّم	*btit3állam*	بْتِتْعَلَّم
hínni	*t3államu*	تْعلَّموا	*yit3államu*	يِتْعَلَّموا	*byit3államu*	بْيِتْعَلَّموا

	imperative	
ínta	*t3állam*	تْعلَّم
ínti	*t3állami*	تْعلَّمي
íntu	*t3államu*	تْعلَّموا

	active participle	
masculine	*mit3állam*	مِتْعلَّم
feminine	*mit3állmi*	مِتْعَلّْمِة
plural	*mit3allmīn*	مِتْعَلّْمين

وِيْن تْعلّمْتوا؟

Where did you study?

ما بدّك تِتْعلّم فرْنْسي؟

Don't you want to study French?

سميرة مِتْعلّْمِة بِيولوجي.

Samira has studied biology.

عم إتْعلّم هنْدسِة كهْربا.

I'm studying electrical engineering.

وْلاد رامي بْيِتْعلّموا بمْدْرسِة خُصوصية.

Rami's children study in a private school.

13 *defective measure V* to have lunch تْغَدّى

	perfect		imperfect		bi-imperfect	
ána	*tɣaddēt*	تْغَدّيْت	*itɣádda*	إتْغَدّى	*bitɣádda*	بْتغَدّى
níḫna	*tɣaddáyna*	تْغَدَّيْنا	*nitɣádda*	نِتْغَدّى	*mnitɣádda*	مْنِتْغَدّى
ínta	*tɣaddēt*	تْغَدّيْت	*titɣádda*	تِتْغَدّى	*btitɣádda*	بْتِتْغَدّى
ínti	*tɣaddáyti*	تْغَدَّيْتي	*titɣáddi*	تِتْغَدّي	*btitɣáddi*	بْتِتْغَدّي
íntu	*tɣaddáytu*	تْغَدَّيْتوا	*titɣáddu*	تِتْغَدّوا	*btitɣáddu*	بْتِتْغَدّوا
húwwi	*tɣádda*	تْغَدّى	*yitɣádda*	يِتْغَدّى	*byitɣádda*	بْيِتْغَدّى
híyyi	*tɣáddit*	تْغَدِّت	*titɣádda*	تِتْغَدّى	*btitɣádda*	بْتِتْغَدّى
hínni	*tɣáddu*	تْغَدّوا	*yitɣáddu*	يِتْغَدّوا	*byitɣáddu*	بْيِتْغَدّوا

	imperative	
ínta	*tɣádda*	تْغَدّى
ínti	*tɣáddi*	تْغَدّي
íntu	*tɣáddu*	تْغَدّوا

	active participle	
masculine	*mitɣáddi*	مِتْغَدّي
feminine	*mitɣaddíyyi*	مِتْغَدّيّة
plural	*mitɣaddyīn*	مِتْغَدّيين

تْغَدَّيْنا مْبارِح بِمْطْعَم وادي شَمْسين.

Yesterday, we had lunch at the restaurant Wadi Chemsine.

عَ بُكْرا حنعْمِل غدا. عْمول حسيبك تِتْغدّى عِنّا.

Tomorrow, we will prepare food. So make sure you come have lunch at our place.

بْتِتْغدّي بْسما بيْروت عالحمْرا بسّ تْخلّص مُحاضرْتِك؟

Would you like to have lunch at Beirut Sky in Hamra after you finish your lecture?

ما تْغدّيْت بعْدك؟

Didn't you eat lunch yet?

تْغدّي هلّق مِنْشان تِقْدري تْكمّلي شِغْلِك.

Eat your lunch now, so you can continue your work.

14 *defective measure VI* **to avoid** تْفادى

	perfect		imperfect		bi-imperfect	
ána	*tfēdēt*	تْفاديْت	*itfēda*	إتْفادى	*bitfēda*	بِتْفادى
níḫna	*tfēdáyna*	تْفاديْنا	*nitfēda*	نِتْفادى	*mnitfēda*	مْنِتْفادى
ínta	*tfēdēt*	تْفاديْت	*titfēda*	تِتْفادى	*btitfēda*	بْتِتْفادى
ínti	*tfēdáyti*	تْفادَيْتي	*titfēdi*	تِتْفادي	*btitfēdi*	بْتِتْفادي
íntu	*tfēdáytu*	تْفادَيْتوا	*titfēdu*	تِتْفادوا	*btitfēdu*	بْتِتْفادوا
húwwi	*tfēda*	تْفادى	*yitfēda*	يِتْفادى	*byitfēda*	بْيِتْفادى
híyyi	*tfēdit*	تْفادِت	*titfēda*	تِتْفادى	*btitfēda*	بْتِتْفادى
hínni	*tfēdu*	تْفادوا	*yitfēdu*	يِتْفادوا	*byitfēdu*	بْيِتْفادوا

	imperative	
ínta	*tfēda*	تْفادى
ínti	*tfēdi*	تْفادي
íntu	*tfēdu*	تْفادوا

	active participle	
masculine	*mitfēdi*	مِتْفادي
feminine	*mitfēdíyyi*	مِتْفادِيّة
plural	*mitfēdyīn*	مِتْفاديين

⚠ The feminine active participle is also commonly pronounced مِتْفادايِة *mitfēdēyi,* as in the fifth example below.

تْفادَيْتوا المشاكِل هَيْدي المرّة.

You got away without trouble this time!

لازِم تِتْفادى تْقرِّب مِن فادي.

You should avoid getting too close to Fadi.

بدْكُن تِتْعلّموا كيف تِتْفادوا تِدْقروا بعْض بْكُرة سلّة.

You should learn how to avoid touching each other in basketball.

ما بْيِتْفادى العجْقة بِالطُّرُقات.

He doesn't avoid traffic.

تانْيا مِتْفادية السُّؤال.

Tania has avoided the question

to err تْلَخْبَط

	perfect		imperfect		bi-imperfect	
ána	tlaxbáṭit	تْلَخْبَطِت	itláxbaṭ	إتْلَخْبَط	bitláxbaṭ	بِتْلَخْبَط
níḫna	tlaxbáṭna	تْلَخْبَطْنا	nitláxbaṭ	نِتْلَخْبَط	mnitláxbaṭ	مْنِتْلَخْبَط
ínta	tlaxbáṭit	تْلَخْبَطِت	titláxbaṭ	تِتْلَخْبَط	btitláxbaṭ	بْتِتْلَخْبَط
ínti	tlaxbáṭti	تْلَخْبَطْتي	titláxbaṭi	تِتْلَخْبَطي	btitláxbaṭi	بْتِتْلَخْبَطي
íntu	tlaxbáṭtu	تْلَخْبَطْتوا	titláxbaṭu	تِتْلَخْبَطوا	btitláxbaṭu	بْتِتْلَخْبَطوا
húwwi	tláxbaṭ	تْلَخْبَط	yitláxbaṭ	يِتْلَخْبَط	byitláxbaṭ	بْيِتْلَخْبَط
híyyi	tláxbaṭit	تْلَخْبَطِت	titláxbaṭ	تِتْلَخْبَط	btitláxbaṭ	بْتِتْلَخْبَط
hínni	tláxbaṭu	تْلَخْبَطوا	yitláxbaṭu	يِتْلَخْبَطوا	byitláxbaṭu	بْيِتْلَخْبَطوا

	imperative	
ínta	láxbiṭ	لَخْبِط
ínti	láxbṭi	لَخْبْطي
íntu	láxbṭu	لَخْبْطوا

	active participle	
masculine	mitláxbaṭ	مِتْلَخْبَط
feminine	mitláxbṭa	مِتْلَخْبْطَة
plural	mitlaxbṭīn	مِتْلَخْبْطين

تْلَخْبطْنا بِالعِنْوان.

We got the address wrong.

ليْه بْتِتْلخْبط دايماً بِالحْسابات؟

Why do you always make accounting mistakes?

ما بْيِتْلخْبْطوا قِدّامْنا بِالشّغِل.

They never make mistakes in front of us at work.

بْرتِّب وْراقي كِرْمال ما إتْلخْبط

I organize my papers to not get confused.

لا ما عِنّا حدا هوْن إسْمو سامي، مِتْلخْبِط بِالنُّمْرة.

No, there is no one by the name of Sami here; you've got the wrong number.

16 *sound measure XI* **to phone** تَلْفَن

	perfect		imperfect		bi-imperfect	
ána	*talfánit*	تَلْفَنِت	*tálfin*	تَلْفِن	*btálfin*	بْتَلْفِن
níħna	*talfánna*	تَلْفَنّا	*ntálfin*	نْتَلْفِن	*mintálfin*	مِنْتَلْفِن
ínta	*talfánit*	تَلْفَنِت	*ttálfin*	تْتَلْفِن	*bittálfin*	بِتْتَلْفِن
ínti	*talfánti*	تَلْفَنْتي	*ttálfni*	تْتَلْفْني	*bittálfni*	بِتْتَلْفْني
íntu	*talfántu*	تَلْفَنْتوا	*ttálfnu*	تْتَلْفْنوا	*bittálfnu*	بِتْتَلْفْنوا
húwwi	*tálfan*	تَلْفَن	*ytálfin*	يْتَلْفِن	*bitálfin*	بيتَلْفِن
híyyi	*tálfanit*	تَلْفَنِت	*ttálfin*	تْتَلْفِن	*bittálfin*	بِتْتَلْفِن
hínni	*tálfanu*	تَلْفَنوا	*ytálfnu*	يْتَلْفْنوا	*bitálfnu*	بيتَلْفْنوا

	imperative	
ínta	*tálfin*	تَلْفِن
ínti	*tálfni*	تَلْفْني
íntu	*tálfnu*	تَلْفْنوا

	active participle	
masculine	*mtálfin*	مْتَلْفِن
feminine	*mtálfni*	مْتَلْفْنِة
plural	*mtalfnīn*	مْتَلْفْنين

تلْفنِت لخالك؟

Did you call your uncle?

عم تلْفِن وما حدا عم بيردّ.

I'm calling and no one is answering.

رح يْتلْفِن لصاحِبْتو عالفايبر.

He will call his girlfriend on Viber [app].

هِنِد، ما تْتلْفْني للدّرك هلّق.

Hind, don't call the police now.

تلْفنوا وفسّروا كِلّ شي.

They've called and explained everything.

17 *defective measure V* **to hope** تْمَنّى

	perfect		imperfect		bi-imperfect	
ána	*tmannēt*	تْمَنّيْت	*itmánna*	إتْمَنّى	*bitmánna*	بِتْمَنّى
níђna	*tmannáyna*	تْمَنَّيْنا	*nitmánna*	نِتْمَنّى	*mnitmánna*	مْنِتْمَنّى
ínta	*tmannēt*	تْمَنّيْت	*titmánna*	تِتْمَنّى	*btitmánna*	بْتِتْمَنّى
ínti	*tmannáyti*	تْمَنَّيْتي	*titmánni*	تِتْمَنّي	*btitmánni*	بْتِتْمَنّي
íntu	*tmannáytu*	تْمَنَّيْتوا	*titmánnu*	تِتْمَنّوا	*btitmánnu*	بْتِتْمَنّوا
húwwi	*tmánna*	تْمَنّى	*yitmánna*	يِتْمَنّى	*byitmánna*	بْيِتْمَنّى
híyyi	*tmánnit*	تْمَنِّت	*titmánna*	تِتْمَنّى	*btitmánna*	بْتِتْمَنّى
hínni	*tmánnu*	تْمَنّوا	*yitmánnu*	يِتْمَنّوا	*byitmánnu*	بْيِتْمَنّوا

	imperative	
ínta	*tmánna*	تْمَنّى
ínti	*tmánni*	تْمَنّي
íntu	*tmánnu*	تْمَنّوا

	active participle	
masculine	*mitmánni*	مِتْمَنّي
feminine	*mitmanníyyi*	مِتْمَنِّيّة
plural	*mitmannyīn*	مِتْمَنّْيين

تْمَنّيْت تِجي مْبارِح عَ السّهْرة.

I hoped you would come last night.

ما بْتِتْمنّي تْصيري مْهنْدْسِة؟

Don’t you hope to become an engineer?

بْيِتْمنّى يْصير مْغنّي.

He hopes to become a singer.

تْمنّوا يْصير بيُّكُن مْنيح.

Have hope that your dad will get well.

مْنِتْمنّى لوَضِع يْروق.

We hope the situation calms down.

18 *hollow measure I* to bring جاب

	perfect		imperfect		bi-imperfect	
ána	*jíbit*	جِبِت	*jīb*	جيب	*bjīb*	بْجيب
níḩna	*jíbna*	جِبْنا	*njīb*	نْجيب	*minjīb*	مِنْجيب
ínta	*jíbit*	جِبِت	*tjīb*	تْجيب	*bitjīb*	بِتْجيب
ínti	*jíbti*	جِبْتي	*tjībi*	تْجيبي	*bitjībi*	بِتْجيبي
íntu	*jíbtu*	جِبْتوا	*tjību*	تْجيبوا	*bitjību*	بِتْجيبوا
húwwi	*jēb*	جاب	*yjīb*	يْجيب	*bijīb*	بيجيب
híyyi	*jēbit*	جابِت	*tjīb*	تْجيب	*bitjīb*	بِتْجيب
hínni	*jēbu*	جابوا	*yjību*	يْجيبوا	*bijību*	بيجيبوا

	imperative	
ínta	*jīb*	جيب
ínti	*jībi*	جيبي
íntu	*jību*	جيبوا

	active participle	
masculine	*jēyib*	جايِب
feminine	*jēybi*	جايْبِة
plural	*jēybīn*	جايْبين

رح جيب قالِب كاتو عالحفْلِة.
I will bring a cake to the party.

ما جِبِت الخبِز؟
Didn't you bring any bread?

جيبي جِزْدانِك معِك.
Bring your handbag with you.

جيب الدَّوا بْطريقك مِن الصَّيْدلية.
Bring the medicine with you from the pharmacy.

جيبوا الأكِل لهون.
Bring the food here.

الجّيران ما جابولْنا غيرْ وَجع الرّاس.
The neighbors only gave us headaches.

رح جيب المصاري مِن البيْت وإنْزِل عالسّوق.
I will bring the money from home and go to market.

رح جيب المْخدِّة ونام عالصوْفا.
I will bring the pillow and sleep on the sofa.

19 *sound measure III* **to try** حاوَل

	perfect		imperfect		bi-imperfect	
ána	*ɦāwálit*	حاوَلت	*ɦāwil*	حاوِل	*bɦāwil*	بْحاوِل
níɦna	*ɦāwálna*	حاوَلْنا	*nɦāwil*	نْحاوِل	*minɦāwil*	مِنْحاوِل
ínta	*ɦāwálit*	حاوَلِت	*tɦāwil*	تْحاوِل	*bitɦāwil*	بِتْحاوِل
ínti	*ɦāwálti*	حاوَلْتي	*tɦāwli*	تْحاوْلي	*bitɦāwli*	بِتْحاوْلي
íntu	*ɦāwáltu*	حاوَلْتوا	*tɦāwlu*	تْحاوْلوا	*bitɦāwlu*	بِتْحاوْلوا
húwwi	*ɦāwal*	حاوَل	*yɦāwil*	يْحاوِل	*biɦāwil*	بيحاوِل
híyyi	*ɦāwalit*	حاوَلِت	*tɦāwil*	تْحاوِل	*bitɦāwil*	بِتْحاوِل
hínni	*ɦāwalu*	حاوَلوا	*yɦāwlu*	يْحاوْلوا	*biɦāwlu*	بيحاوْلوا

	imperative	
ínta	*ɦāwil*	حاوِل
ínti	*ɦāwli*	حاوْلي
íntu	*ɦāwlu*	حاوْلوا

	active participle	
masculine	*mɦāwil*	مْحاوِل
feminine	*mɦāwli*	مْحاوْلِة
plural	*mɦāwlīn*	مْحاوْلين

حاوَلْتوا تْحِلّوا هاللِّغِز!

Did you try to solve this mystery!

ما عم تْحاوِل تعْمِل شي بْحَياتك!

You're not trying to do anything in life!

كْتير بِتْحاوِل تِخْسر وَزِن مِنْشان صحِّتا.

She is trying hard to lose weight for the sake of her health.

حاوْلوا تِشْتِغْلوا سَوا.

Try to work together.

عم يْحاوِل يْظبِّط وَضْعو مع المُدير.

He is trying to be friends with the manager.

20 *geminate measure I* **to like** حَبّ

	perfect		imperfect		bi-imperfect	
ána	*ɧabbēt*	حَبّيْت	*ɧibb*	حِبّ	*bɧibb*	بْحِبّ
níɧna	*ɧabbáyna*	حَبَّيْنا	*nɧibb*	نْحِبّ	*minɧíbb*	مِنْحِبّ
ínta	*ɧabbēt*	حَبَّيْت	*tɧibb*	تْحِبّ	*bitɧíbb*	بِتْحِبّ
ínti	*ɧabbáyti*	حَبَّيْتي	*tɧíbbi*	تْحِبّي	*bitɧíbbi*	بِتْحِبّي
íntu	*ɧabbáytu*	حَبَّيْتوا	*tɧíbbu*	تْحِبّوا	*bitɧíbbu*	بِتْحِبّوا
húwwi	*ɧabb*	حَبّ	*yɧibb*	يْحِبّ	*biɧíbb*	بيحِبّ
híyyi	*ɧábbit*	حَبِّت	*tɧibb*	تْحِبّ	*bitɧíbb*	بِتْحِبّ
hínni	*ɧábbu*	حَبّوا	*yɧíbbu*	يْحِبّوا	*biɧíbbu*	بيحِبّوا

	imperative	
ínta	*ɧibb*	حِبّ
ínti	*ɧíbbi*	حِبّي
íntu	*ɧíbbu*	حِبّوا

	active participle	
masculine	*ɧābib*	حابِب
feminine	*ɧābbi*	حابّة
plural	*ɧābbīn*	حابّين

⚠ The long vowel in a measure-I active participle is more commonly *ē*. In this particular verb, it is pronounced *ā* because it follows *ɧ*.

ما حبّيْت خبرْك قُصّتي.

I didn't want to tell you my story.

بِتْحِبّ تِشْرب قهْوِة معي؟

Would you like to drink some coffee with me?

بِتْحِبّ الشّوكولا والشّيبْس كْتير.

She really likes chocolate and potato chips.

مِنْحِبّ نْروح نِتْسوّق ونِحْضر سينِما.

We like to go shopping and to the movies.

كِنِت حابِب أعْمِل تمْريض.

I wanted to go into nursing.

21 *sound measure VIII* **to celebrate** حْتَفَل

	perfect		imperfect		bi-imperfect	
ána	*ḫtafálit*	حْتَفَلت	*íḫtifil*	إحْتِفِل	*bíḫtifil*	بِحْتِفِل
níḫna	*ḫtafálna*	حْتَفَلْنا	*níḫtifil*	نِحْتِفِل	*mníḫtifil*	مْنِحْتِفِل
ínta	*ḫtafálit*	حْتَفَلت	*tíḫtifil*	تِحْتِفِل	*btíḫtifil*	بْتِحْتِفِل
ínti	*ḫtafálti*	حْتَفَلْتي	*tiḫtífli*	تِحْتِفْلي	*btiḫtífli*	بْتِحْتِفْلي
íntu	*ḫtafáltu*	حْتَفَلْتوا	*tiḫtíflu*	تِحْتِفْلوا	*btiḫtíflu*	بْتِحْتِفْلوا
húwwi	*ḫtáfal*	حْتَفَل	*yíḫtifil*	يِحْتِفِل	*byíḫtifil*	بْيِحْتِفِل
híyyi	*ḫtáfalit*	حْتَفَلت	*tíḫtifil*	تِحْتِفِل	*btíḫtifil*	بْتِحْتِفِل
hínni	*ḫtáfalu*	حْتَفَلوا	*yiḫtíflu*	يِحْتِفْلوا	*byiḫtíflu*	بْيِحْتِفْلوا

	imperative	
ínta	*ḫtífil*	حْتِفِل
ínti	*ḫtífli*	حْتِفْلي
íntu	*ḫtíflu*	حْتِفْلوا

	active participle	
masculine	*míḫtifil*	مِحْتِفِل
feminine	*miḫtífli*	مِحْتِفْلة
plural	*miḫtiflīn*	مِحْتِفْلين

حْتفلْنا بْعيد ميلاد البابا بْشْباط.

We celebrated dad’s birthday in February.

رح إحْتِفِل بْعيد العِشّاق هالسِّنِة.

I will celebrate Valentine’s Day this year.

رايْحين نِحْتِفِل بْتخرُّج إبن عَمّْنا حسن.

We’re going to celebrate our cousin Hassan’s graduation.

هالسِّنِة العالم مِش مِحْتِفْلين بْمهرجان بيرْوت السّينِمائي كالعادِة.

This year, people are not celebrating the Beirut Film Festival as usual.

يَلّا حْتِفْلي بِالبيْبي الجْديد.

Come on, celebrate the newborn baby.

22 *sound measure II* **to move** حَرَّك

	perfect		imperfect		bi-imperfect	
ána	*ђarrákit*	حَرَّكِت	*ђárrik*	حَرِّك	*bђárrik*	بْحَرِّك
níђna	*ђarrákna*	حَرَّكْنا	*nђárrik*	نْحَرِّك	*minђárrik*	مِنْحَرِّك
ínta	*ђarrákit*	حَرَّكِت	*tђárrik*	تْحَرِّك	*bitђárrik*	بِتْحَرِّك
ínti	*ђarrákti*	حَرَّكْتي	*tђárrki*	تْحَرّْكي	*bitђárrki*	بِتْحَرّْكي
íntu	*ђarráktu*	حَرَّكْتوا	*tђárrku*	تْحَرّْكوا	*bitђárrku*	بِتْحَرّْكوا
húwwi	*ђárrak*	حَرَّك	*yђárrik*	يْحَرِّك	*biђárrik*	بيحَرِّك
híyyi	*ђárrakit*	حَرَّكِت	*tђárrik*	تْحَرِّك	*bitђárrik*	بِتْحَرِّك
hínni	*ђárraku*	حَرَّكوا	*yђárrku*	يْحَرّْكوا	*biђárrku*	بيحَرّْكوا

	imperative	
ínta	*ђárrik*	حَرِّك
ínti	*ђárrki*	حَرّْكي
íntu	*ђárrku*	حَرّْكوا

	active participle	
masculine	*mђárrik*	مْحَرِّك
feminine	*mђárrki*	مْحَرّْكِة
plural	*mђárrkīn*	مْحَرّْكين

بسّ أَيْمن ورنْدة حرّكوا جَوّ الحفْلِة.

Ayman and Randa are the life of the party.

ما فيك تْحرِّك حالك شْوَيّ أسْرع؟

Can't you move any faster?

شو قَوْلِك ماما، بْحرِّك الطّبْخة ولّا بْنْطر؟

What do you think, Mom? Should I stir the food or wait?

حرِّك معي هالطّاوْلِة لنحطّا بِالجْنيْنة.

Come help me move this table to the garden.

حرّْكي إجْرِك أحْسن ما تْنمِّل!

Move your leg so it doesn't get numb!

geminate measure I — to feel — حَسّ

	perfect		imperfect		bi-imperfect	
ána	ɧassēt	حَسّيْت	ɧiss	حِسّ	bɧiss	بْحِسّ
níɧna	ɧassáyna	حَسَّيْنا	nɧiss	نْحِسّ	minɧiss	مِنْحِسّ
ínta	ɧassēt	حَسّيْت	tɧiss	تْحِسّ	bitɧíss	بِتْحِسّ
ínti	ɧassáyti	حَسَّيْتي	tɧíssi	تْحِسّي	bitɧíssi	بِتْحِسّي
íntu	ɧassáytu	حَسَّيْتوا	tɧíssu	تْحِسّوا	bitɧíssu	بِتْحِسّوا
húwwi	ɧass	حَسّ	yɧiss	يْحِسّ	biɧíss	بيحِسّ
híyyi	ɧássit	حَسِّت	tɧiss	تْحِسّ	bitɧíss	بِتْحِسّ
hínni	ɧássu	حَسّوا	yɧíssu	يْحِسّوا	biɧíssu	بيحِسّوا

	imperative	
ínta	ɧiss	حِسّ
ínti	ɧíssi	حِسّي
íntu	ɧíssu	حِسّوا

	active participle	
masculine	ɧēsis	حاسِس
feminine	ɧēssi	حاسِّة
plural	ɧēssīn	حاسّين

بِتْحِسّ ما في حدا بيحِبّا.
She feels that no one loves her.

بْحِسّ إنّي بِقْدر خلِّص هالمُهِمّة.
I feel that I can do this task.

كيف حاسِس حالك مِن بعْد ما أخدِت الْدّوا؟
How do you feel after taking the medicine?

بِتْحِسّي بِالوَجع بِاللّيْل ما هيْك؟
You feel the pain at night, right?

حاسِّة المَوْضوع فيه شكّ؟
Do you doubt the story?

ما عم يْحِسّوا عَ حالُن بسّ يِحْكوا بْصوْت عالي.
They don't notice when they're talking loudly.

to watch حِضِر

	perfect		imperfect		bi-imperfect	
ána	*ɦdírit*	حْضِرت	*íɦdar*	إِحْضَر	*bíɦdar*	بِحْضَر
níɦna	*ɦdírna*	حْضِرْنا	*níɦdar*	نِحْضَر	*mníɦdar*	مْنِحْضَر
ínta	*ɦdírit*	حْضِرت	*tíɦdar*	تِحْضَر	*btíɦdar*	بْتِحْضَر
ínti	*ɦdírti*	حْضِرْتي	*tíɦdari*	تِحْضَري	*btíɦdari*	بْتِحْضَري
íntu	*ɦdírtu*	حْضِرْتوا	*tíɦdaru*	تِحْضَروا	*btíɦdaru*	بْتِحْضَروا
húwwi	*ɦídir*	حِضِر	*yíɦdar*	يِحْضَر	*byíɦdar*	بْيِحْضَر
híyyi	*ɦídrit*	حِضْرت	*tíɦdar*	تِحْضَر	*btíɦdar*	بْتِحْضَر
hínni	*ɦídru*	حِضْروا	*yíɦdaru*	يِحْضَروا	*byíɦdaru*	بْيِحْضَروا

	imperative	
ínta	*ɦdār*	حْضار
ínti	*ɦdári*	حْضَري
íntu	*ɦdáru*	حْضَروا

	active participle	
masculine	*ɦādir*	حاضِر
feminine	*ɦādra*	حاضْرَة
plural	*ɦādrīn*	حاضْرين

حْضِرْنا فيلْم كْتير حِلْو بِالسّينِما.

We watched a really good movie at the cinema.

ما بدّي إجي هلّق لأنّي قاعِد عم إحْضر الماتْش.

I don't want to come now because I'm watching the soccer match.

شِفْتا مْدوّْرة التِّلِفزْيوْن وعم تِحْضر فيلْم.

I saw her with the TV on, watching a movie.

ما بْتِحْضَروا مُسلْسلات لِبْنانية؟

Don't you watch Lebanese series?

حاضْرين حفْلِة تخرُّج لميس ووِسام.

They have attended Lamis and Wissam's graduation party.

to put حَطّ

	perfect		imperfect		bi-imperfect	
ána	*ḫattēt*	حَطّيْت	*ḫutt*	حُطّ	*bḫutt*	بْحُطّ
níḫna	*ḫattáyna*	حَطّيْنا	*nḫutt*	نْحُطّ	*minḫútt*	مِنْحُطّ
ínta	*ḫattēt*	حَطّيْت	*tḫutt*	تْحُطّ	*bitḫútt*	بِتْحُطّ
ínti	*ḫattáyti*	حَطّيْتي	*tḫútti*	تْحُطّي	*bitḫútti*	بِتْحُطّي
íntu	*ḫattáytu*	حَطّيْتوا	*tḫúttu*	تْحُطّوا	*bitḫúttu*	بِتْحُطّوا
húwwi	*ḫatt*	حَطّ	*yḫutt*	يْحُطّ	*biḫútt*	بيحُطّ
híyyi	*ḫáttit*	حَطِّت	*tḫutt*	تْحُطّ	*bitḫútt*	بِتْحُطّ
hínni	*ḫáttu*	حَطّوا	*yḫúttu*	يْحُطّوا	*biḫúttu*	بيحُطّوا

	imperative	
ínta	*ḫutt*	حُطّ
ínti	*ḫútti*	حُطّي
íntu	*ḫúttu*	حُطّوا

	active participle	
masculine	*ḫātit*	حاطِط
feminine	*ḫātta*	حاطّة
plural	*ḫāttīn*	حاطّين

⚠ Some speakers pronounce this particular verb with ◌َ *a* in the imperfect: يْحَطّ *yḫatt*. Other **1g2** verbs (➲ *p. 125*) normally take ◌ُ *u*.

مْبارِح حطّوا مُباشر المُظاهرات اللي صارِت بْقلْب البلد.

Yesterday, they broadcast the demonstrations that happened downtown live on TV.

ليْه بِتْحطّوا هاي الاذاعة دايْماً؟

Why do you always put on the same channel?

بْحِبّ حُطّ وَرد عَ طاوْلِة المطبْخ.

I like to place flowers on the kitchen table.

حاطّة مكْياج كْتير عَ وِجّا.

She has put a lot of makeup on her face.

حُطّ حالك محلّي قبل ما تْقرِّر شو لازِم أعْمِل!

Put yourself in my place before you decide what I should do!

حُطّي البيتْزا بِالفِرن.

Put the pizza in the oven.

26 *defective measure I* **to speak** حِكي

	perfect		imperfect		bi-imperfect	
ána	*ɦkīt*	حْكيت	*íɦki*	إِحْكي	*bíɦki*	بِحْكي
níɦna	*ɦkīna*	حْكينا	*níɦki*	نِحْكي	*mníɦki*	مْنِحْكي
ínta	*ɦkīt*	حْكيت	*tíɦki*	تِحْكي	*btíɦki*	بْتِحْكي
ínti	*ɦkīti*	حْكيتي	*tíɦki*	تِحْكي	*btíɦki*	بْتِحْكي
íntu	*ɦkītu*	حْكيتوا	*tíɦku*	تِحْكوا	*btíɦku*	بْتِحْكوا
húwwi	*ɦíki*	حِكي	*yíɦki*	يِحْكي	*byíɦki*	بْيِحْكي
híyyi	*ɦíkyit*	حِكْيِت	*tíɦki*	تِحْكي	*btíɦki*	بْتِحْكي
hínni	*ɦíkyu*	حِكْيوا	*yíɦku*	يِحْكوا	*byíɦku*	بْيِحْكوا

	imperative	
ínta	*ɦkī*	حْكي
ínti	*ɦkī*	حْكي
íntu	*ɦkū*	حْكوا

	active participle	
masculine	*ɦēki*	حاكي
feminine	*ɦēkyi*	حاكْيِة
plural	*ɦēkyīn*	حاكْيين

حْكينا معُن لساعات.

We talked to them for hours.

عن شو عم تِحْكوا؟

What are you talking about?

بْتِحْكي إنْكْليزي؟

Do you speak English?

حْكي القُصّة اللي خبرّْتْني ياها مْبارِح.

Tell him the story you told me yesterday.

رح إحْكي عن المشْكل بِالاِجْتِماع بُكْرا.

I'll talk about the problem at the meeting tomorrow.

sound measure IX

to become red

حْمَرّ

	perfect		imperfect		bi-imperfect	
ána	*ɦmarrēt*	حْمَرّيْت	*iɦmárr*	إحْمَرّ	*biɦmárr*	بِحْمَرّ
níɦna	*ɦmarráyna*	حْمَرَّيْنا	*niɦmárr*	نِحْمَرّ	*mniɦmárr*	مْنِحْمَرّ
ínta	*ɦmarrēt*	حْمَرّيْت	*tiɦmárr*	تِحْمَرّ	*btiɦmárr*	بْتِحْمَرّ
ínti	*ɦmarráyti*	حْمَرَّيْتي	*tiɦmárri*	تِحْمَرّي	*btiɦmárri*	بْتِحْمَرّي
íntu	*ɦmarráytu*	حْمَرَّيْتوا	*tiɦmárru*	تِحْمَرّوا	*btiɦmárru*	بْتِحْمَرّوا
húwwi	*ɦmarr*	حْمَرّ	*yiɦmárr*	يِحْمَرّ	*byiɦmárr*	بْيِحْمَرّ
híyyi	*ɦmárrit*	حْمَرِّت	*tiɦmárr*	تِحْمَرّ	*btiɦmárr*	بْتِحْمَرّ
hínni	*ɦmárru*	حْمَرّوا	*yiɦmárru*	يِحْمَرّوا	*byiɦmárru*	بْيِحْمَرّوا

	imperative	
ínta	*ɦmarr*	حْمَرّ
ínti	*ɦmárri*	حْمَرّي
íntu	*ɦmárru*	حْمَرّوا

	active participle	
masculine	*miɦmárr*	مِحْمَرّ
feminine	*miɦmárra*	مِحْمَرَّة
plural	*miɦmarrīn*	مِحْمَرّين

حْمَرّ وِجّي مِن الخجل.

I blushed out of embarrassment.

لمّا شافْني حْمرّوا خْدودو.

When he saw me, his cheeks turned red.

بْيِحْمْرّوا إيديه مِن البرد.

My hands turn red from the cold.

حْمَرِّت السّما لمّا غابِت الشّمِس.

The sky turned red when the sun went down.

الشّاشِة حْمرِّت، بعْديْن زْرقِّت وبِالأخير صْفرِّت.

The screen turned red, then blue, then yellow.

sound measure I — to stop — خِلِص

	perfect		imperfect		bi-imperfect	
ána	xlíṣit	خْلِصِت	íxlaṣ	إِخْلَص	bíxlaṣ	بِخْلَص
níḫna	xlíṣna	خْلِصْنا	níxlaṣ	نِخْلَص	mníxlaṣ	مْنِخْلَص
ínta	xlíṣit	خْلِصِت	tíxlaṣ	تِخْلَص	btíxlaṣ	بْتِخْلَص
ínti	xlíṣti	خْلِصْتي	tíxlaṣi	تِخلَصي	btíxlaṣi	بْتِخْلَصي
íntu	xlíṣtu	خْلِصْتوا	tíxlaṣu	تِخلَصوا	btíxlaṣu	بْتِخْلَصوا
húwwi	xíliṣ	خِلِص	yíxlaṣ	يِخلَص	byíxlaṣ	بْيِخْلَص
híyyi	xílṣit	خِلْصِت	tíxlaṣ	تِخلَص	btíxlaṣ	بْتِخْلَص
hínni	xílṣu	خِلْصوا	yíxlaṣu	يِخلَصوا	byíxlaṣu	بْيِخْلَصوا

	imperative	
ínta	xlāṣ	خْلاص
ínti	xláṣi	خْلَصي
íntu	xláṣu	خْلَصوا

	active participle	
masculine	xāliṣ	خالِص
feminine	xālṣa	خالْصَة
plural	xālṣīn	خالْصين

خِلْصِت الحفْلِة بْسبب المشْكل.

The party stopped because the fight.

خْلصي مِن التّفْكير بْهالشّغْلِة.

Stop thinking about that.

إذا بْتِترْكيه، بْيِخْلص حكْيو معِك.

If you break up with him, he'll stop talking to you.

خِلِص المِشْوار لأنّ تِعِبْنا.

The journey stopped because we were tired

هَيْدول الجّماعة خالْصين مِن كْتِـر الشُّرْب.

These people are wasted from drinking too much.

29 *sound measure II* to finish خَلَّص

	perfect		imperfect		bi-imperfect	
ána	*xalláṣit*	خَلَّصت	*xálliṣ*	خَلِّص	*bxálliṣ*	بْخَلِّص
níḫna	*xalláṣna*	خَلَّصْنا	*nxálliṣ*	نْخَلِّص	*minxálliṣ*	مِنْخَلِّص
ínta	*xalláṣit*	خَلَّصت	*txálliṣ*	تْخَلِّص	*bitxálliṣ*	بِتْخَلِّص
ínti	*xalláṣti*	خَلَّصْتي	*txállṣi*	تْخَلّْصي	*bitxállṣi*	بِتْخَلّْصي
íntu	*xalláṣtu*	خَلَّصْتوا	*txállṣu*	تْخَلّْصوا	*bitxállṣu*	بِتْخَلّْصوا
húwwi	*xállaṣ*	خَلَّص	*yxálliṣ*	يْخَلِّص	*bixálliṣ*	بيخَلِّص
híyyi	*xállaṣit*	خَلَّصت	*txálliṣ*	تْخَلِّص	*bitxálliṣ*	بِتْخَلِّص
hínni	*xállaṣu*	خَلَّصوا	*yxállṣu*	يْخَلّْصوا	*bixállṣu*	بيخَلّْصوا

	imperative	
ínta	*xálliṣ*	خَلِّص
ínti	*xállṣi*	خَلّْصي
íntu	*xállṣu*	خَلّْصوا

	active participle	
masculine	*mxálliṣ*	مْخَلِّص
feminine	*mxállṣa*	مْخَلّْصَة
plural	*mxallṣīn*	مْخَلّْصين

أَيْمتى خلّصْتوا الامْتِحانات؟

When did you finish the exams?

دايمًا بْخلِّص شِغْلي عالسّاعة ٥.

I always finish my work at five o'clock.

عبِد إذا لزق فيك ما بِتْخلِّص مِنّو.

You can never get rid of Abed once he clings to you.

يَلّا سامْيَة خلّْصي اِللي بْإيدِك والْحقيني.

Come on, Samia. Finish what you're doing and follow me.

مْخلِّص دْروسو عَ بكّير.

He finished his homework early.

30 *defective measure II* **to let** خَلّى

	perfect		imperfect		bi-imperfect	
ána	*xallēt*	خَلّيْت	*xálli*	خَلّي	*bxálli*	بْخَلّي
níħna	*xalláyna*	خَلَّيْنا	*nxálli*	نْخَلّي	*minxálli*	مِنْخَلّي
ínta	*xallēt*	خَلّيْت	*txálli*	تْخَلّي	*bitxálli*	بِتْخَلّي
ínti	*xalláyti*	خَلَّيْتي	*txálli*	تْخَلّي	*bitxálli*	بِتْخَلّي
íntu	*xalláytu*	خَلَّيْتوا	*txállu*	تْخَلّوا	*bitxállu*	بِتْخَلّوا
húwwi	*xálla*	خَلّى	*yxálli*	يْخَلّي	*bixálli*	بيخَلّي
híyyi	*xállit*	خَلِّت	*txálli*	تْخَلّي	*bitxálli*	بِتْخَلّي
hínni	*xállu*	خَلّوا	*yxállu*	يْخَلّوا	*bixállu*	بيخَلّوا

	imperative	
ínta	*xálli*	خَلّي
ínti	*xálli*	خَلّي
íntu	*xállu*	خَلّوا

	active participle	
masculine	*mxálli*	مْخَلّي
feminine	*mxállyi*	مخَلّية
plural	*mxallyīn*	مخَلّيين

ليْه ما خلِّت محطّة الأخْبار تعْمِل مُقابلة معْنا؟
Why didn't she let the news channel interview us?

خلّي هاني يِحْكي قُصّتو.
Make Hanny tell his story.

بِتْحِبّ تْخلّي صُوَرك معي؟
Would you like to keep your photos with me?

بِتْخلّي البِسايْنات برّات البيْت؟
Do you keep the cats outside the house?

خالْتو، فيكي تْخلّي مُحمّد يِجي معي؟
Aunt, can you let Mohamad come with me?

 sound measure I

to study دَرَس

	perfect		imperfect		bi-imperfect	
ána	*darásit*	دَرَسِت	*ídrus*	إِدْرُس	*bídrus*	بِدْرُس
níḫna	*darásna*	دَرَسْنا	*nídrus*	نِدْرُس	*mnídrus*	مْنِدْرُس
ínta	*darásit*	دَرَسِت	*tídrus*	تِدْرُس	*btídrus*	بْتِدْرُس
ínti	*darásti*	دَرَسْتي	*tídirsi*	تِدِرْسي	*btídirsi*	بْتِدِرْسي
íntu	*darástu*	دَرَسْتوا	*tídirsu*	تِدِرْسوا	*btídirsu*	بْتِدِرْسوا
húwwi	*dáras*	دَرَس	*yídrus*	يِدْرُس	*byídrus*	بْيِدْرُس
híyyi	*dárasit*	دَرَسِت	*tídrus*	تِدْرُس	*btídrus*	بْتِدْرُس
hínni	*dárasu*	دَرَسوا	*yídirsu*	يِدِرْسوا	*byídirsu*	بْيِدِرْسوا

	imperative	
ínta	*drūs*	دْروس
ínti	*drísi*	دْرِسي
íntu	*drísu*	دْرِسوا

	active participle	
masculine	*dēris*	دارِس
feminine	*dērsi*	دارْسِة
plural	*dērsīn*	دارْسين

رِحْنا نِدْرُس عِنْد جيْهان.
We went to study at Jehan's place.

درسِت لِلامْتِحانات مْنيح.
She studied hard for the exams.

عُمر ما بْيِدْرُس بسّ يِرْجع مِن المدْرسِة. ما بعْرف كيف بْيِنْجح!
Omar never studies when he gets back from school. I don't know how he'll pass!

دْرِسي يا نانْسي كِرْمال تِنْجحي بِالاِخْتِبار.
Nancy, study so you can pass your tests.

بْتِدِرْسوا سَوا لمّا تْفِلّوا عالبيْت.
Study together when you get home.

32 *sound measure I* **to pay** دَفَع

	perfect		imperfect		bi-imperfect	
ána	*dafá3it*	دَفَعِت	*ídfa3*	إِدْفَع	*bídfa3*	بِدْفَع
níḫna	*dafá3na*	دَفَعنا	*nídfa3*	نِدْفَع	*mnídfa3*	مْنِدْفَع
ínta	*dafá3it*	دَفَعت	*tídfa3*	تِدْفَع	*btídfa3*	بْتِدْفَع
ínti	*dafá3ti*	دَفَعتي	*tídfa3i*	تِدْفَعي	*btídfa3i*	بْتِدْفَعي
íntu	*dafá3tu*	دَفَعتوا	*tídfa3u*	تِدْفَعوا	*btídfa3u*	بْتِدْفَعوا
húwwi	*dáfa3*	دَفَع	*yídfa3*	يِدْفَع	*byídfa3*	بْيِدْفَع
híyyi	*dáfa3it*	دَفَعت	*tídfa3*	تِدْفَع	*btídfa3*	بْتِدْفَع
hínni	*dáfa3u*	دَفَعوا	*yídfa3u*	يِدْفَعوا	*byídfa3u*	بْيِدْفَعوا

	imperative	
ínta	*dfā3*	دْفاع
ínti	*dfá3i*	دْفَعي
íntu	*dfá3u*	دْفَعوا

	active participle	
masculine	*dēfi3*	دافع
feminine	*dēf3a*	دافْعَة
plural	*dēf3īn*	دافْعين

الزُّبون دفع الفاتورة بِالفيزا كارْد.

The customer paid his bill by Visa card.

بْيِدْفع فَواتيرو عالوَقِت دايماً.

He always pays his bills on time.

بسّ إرْجع مِن شِغْلي بمُرّ عليْك وبِدْفع باقي القِسِط.

When I'm on my way back from work,
I will stop by and pay you the remaining amount.

دفعِت أجار البيْت اليوْم الصُّبُح.

I just paid my rent this morning.

هَيْدول الشّباب بعْدُن ما دافْعين حقّ السنْدِويتْشات.

These guys haven't paid for their sandwiches yet.

33 *sound measure I* to touch دَقَر

	perfect		imperfect		bi-imperfect	
ána	*daʔárit*	دَقَرت	*ídʔar*	إِدْقَر	*bídʔar*	بِدْقَر
níħna	*daʔárna*	دَقَرْنا	*nídʔar*	نِدْقَر	*mnídʔar*	مْنِدْقَر
ínta	*daʔárit*	دَقَرت	*tídʔar*	تِدْقَر	*btídʔar*	بْتِدْقَر
ínti	*daʔárti*	دَقَرْتي	*tídʔari*	تِدْقَري	*btídʔari*	بْتِدْقَري
íntu	*daʔártu*	دَقَرْتوا	*tídʔaru*	تِدْقَروا	*btídʔaru*	بْتِدْقَروا
húwwi	*dáʔar*	دَقَر	*yídʔar*	يِدْقَر	*byídʔar*	بْيِدْقَر
híyyi	*dáʔarit*	دَقَرت	*tídʔar*	تِدْقَر	*btídʔar*	بْتِدْقَر
hínni	*dáʔaru*	دَقَروا	*yídʔaru*	يِدْقَروا	*byídʔaru*	بْيِدْقَروا

	imperative	
ínta	*dʔār*	دْقار
ínti	*dʔári*	دْقَري
íntu	*dʔáru*	دْقَروا

	active participle	
masculine	*dēʔir*	داقِر
feminine	*dēʔra*	داقْرَة
plural	*dēʔrīn*	داقْرين

دقرت سِلْك كهْربا مْظلّط بِالغلط وتْكهْربِت.

I touched an exposed electrical wire by mistake, and I got an electric shock.

ما تِدْقر فِيي!

Don't touch me!

ما بعْرف ليْش الضّيوف ما بْيِدْقروا صحِن الفْواكِه.

I don't know why the guests don't come near the plate of fruit.

دْقري هَيْدا الإقْماش وحِسّيه.

Touch this cloth and feel it.

ما بيحِبْني إدْقر غْراضو.

He doesn't like me to touch his belongings.

34 *hollow measure I* **to go** راح

	perfect		imperfect		bi-imperfect	
ána	*ríħit*	رِحِت	*rūħ*	روح	*brūħ*	بْروح
níħna	*ríħna*	رِحْنا	*nrūħ*	نْروح	*minrūħ*	مِنْروح
ínta	*ríħit*	رِحِت	*trūħ*	تْروح	*bitrūħ*	بِتْروح
ínti	*ríħti*	رِحْتي	*trūħi*	تْروحي	*bitrūħi*	بِتْروحي
íntu	*ríħtu*	رِحْتوا	*trūħu*	تْروحوا	*bitrūħu*	بِتْروحوا
húwwi	*rāħ*	راح	*yrūħ*	يْروح	*birūħ*	بيروح
híyyi	*rāħit*	راحِت	*trūħ*	تْروح	*bitrūħ*	بِتْروح
hínni	*rāħu*	راحوا	*yrūħu*	يْروحوا	*birūħu*	بيروحوا

	imperative	
ínta	*rūħ*	روح
ínti	*rūħi*	روحي
íntu	*rūħu*	روحوا

	active participle	
masculine	*rāyiħ*	رايِح
feminine	*rāyħa*	رايْحَة
plural	*rāyħīn*	رايْحين

وِيْن رايْحة؟

Where are you going?

سامِر ونريمان راحوا على طْرابْلُس مِن أُسْبوع.

Samer and Nariman went to Tripoli a week ago.

ما رِحْنا عالشِّغِل مْبارِح.

We didn't go to work yesterday.

بِدّي روح معك.

I want to go with you.

ما تْروح لَوَحْدك لَهونيْك.

Don't go there by yourself.

عبودي بيروح عالمدْرسِة مِن الصُّبْح.

Aboudi goes to school early in the morning.

to bind رَبَط

	perfect		imperfect		bi-imperfect	
ána	rabáṭit	رَبَطِت	úrbuṭ	أُرْبُط	búrbuṭ	بُرْبُط
níḫna	rabáṭna	رَبَطْنا	núrbuṭ	نُرْبُط	mnúrbuṭ	مْنُرْبُط
ínta	rabáṭit	رَبَطِت	túrbuṭ	تُرْبُط	btúrbuṭ	بْتُرْبُط
ínti	rabáṭti	رَبَطْتي	túrbṭi	تُرْبْطي	btúrbṭi	بْتُرْبْطي
íntu	rabáṭtu	رَبَطْتوا	túrbṭu	تُرْبْطوا	btúrbṭu	بْتُرْبْطوا
húwwi	rábaṭ	رَبَط	yúrbuṭ	يُرْبُط	byúrbuṭ	بْيُرْبُط
híyyi	rábaṭit	رَبَطِت	túrbuṭ	تُرْبُط	btúrbuṭ	بْتُرْبُط
hínni	rábaṭu	رَبَطوا	yúrbṭu	يُرْبْطوا	byúrbṭu	بْيُرْبْطوا

	imperative	
ínta	rbūṭ	رْبوط
ínti	rbúṭi	رْبُطي
íntu	rbúṭu	رْبُطوا

	active participle	
masculine	rābiṭ	رابِط
feminine	rābṭa	رابْطَة
plural	rābṭīn	رابْطين

ربطْنا الألْواح والبالونات عالشّجر.

We tied the banners and balloons on trees.

عم أُرْبُط ربْطِةْ الخِبز.

I'm tying the bread bag.

ما تُرْبُط حالك بمْواعيد كْتيرة.

Don't commit yourself to many appointments.

رْبُطي كيس الزْبالِة وكُبّيه برّا.

Tie the garbage bag and throw it outside.

رْبوط زِنْدك!

Hold your horses! [lit. Tie your wrist!]

كان رابِط البسْكليتّ عالشّجرة.

He had chained the bicycle to the tree.

to rest رْتاح

	perfect		imperfect		bi-imperfect	
ána	rtēħit	رْتاحِت	irtēħ	إرْتاح	birtēħ	بِرْتاح
níħna	rtēħna	رْتاحْنا	nirtēħ	نِرْتاح	mnirtēħ	مْنِرتاح
ínta	rtēħit	رْتاحِت	tirtēħ	تِرْتاح	btirtēħ	بْتِرتاح
ínti	rtēħti	رْتاحْتي	tirtēħi	تِرْتاحي	btirtēħi	بْتِرتاحي
íntu	rtēħtu	رْتاحْتوا	tirtēħu	تِرْتاحوا	btirtēħu	بْتِرتاحوا
húwwi	rtēħ	رْتاح	yirtēħ	يِرْتاح	byirtēħ	بْيِرتاح
híyyi	rtēħit	رْتاحِت	tirtēħ	تِرْتاح	btirtēħ	بْتِرتاح
hínni	rtēħu	رْتاحوا	yirtēħu	يِرْتاحوا	byirtēħu	بْيِرتاحوا

	imperative	
ínta	rtēħ	رْتاح
ínti	rtēħi	رْتاحي
íntu	rtēħu	رْتاحوا

	active participle	
masculine	mirtēħ	مِرْتاح
feminine	mirtēħa	مِرْتاحَة
plural	mirtēħīn	مِرْتاحين

رْتاح بعْد شِغْلك.

Take a rest after your work.

بْحِبّ روح عالمسْبح كِرْمال إرْتاح مِن وَجع الرّاس.

I like to go to the pool to get a peace of mind.

ما بدِّك تِرْتاحي شْوَيّ مِن الكِتابِة؟

Don't you want to take a break from writing?

هالعَيْلِة مِرْتاحين بْحَياتُن.

This family is quite well-off [lit. relaxing in life].

بْتِرتاحوا بسّ توصلوا مْن السّفر.

You will rest when you arrive at your destination [from traveling].

to return رِجِع

	perfect		imperfect		bi-imperfect	
ána	*rjí3it*	رْجِعِت	*írja3*	إِرْجَع	*bírja3*	بِرْجَع
níḫna	*rjí3na*	رْجِعْنا	*nírja3*	نِرْجَع	*mnírja3*	مْنِـرجَع
ínta	*rjí3it*	رْجِعِت	*tírja3*	تِرْجَع	*btírja3*	بْتِـرجَع
ínti	*rjí3ti*	رْجِعْتي	*tírja3i*	تِرْجَعي	*btírja3i*	بْتِـرجَعي
íntu	*rjí3tu*	رْجِعْتوا	*tírja3u*	تِرْجَعوا	*btírja3u*	بْتِـرجَعوا
húwwi	*ríji3*	رِجِع	*yírja3*	يِرْجَع	*byírja3*	بْيِـرجَع
híyyi	*ríj3it*	رِجْعِت	*tírja3*	تِرْجَع	*btírja3*	بْتِـرجَع
hínni	*ríj3u*	رِجْعوا	*yírja3u*	يِرْجَعوا	*byírja3u*	بْيِـرجَعوا

	imperative	
ínta	*rjā3*	رْجاع
ínti	*rjá3i*	رْجَعي
íntu	*rjá3u*	رْجَعوا

	active participle	
masculine	*rēji3*	راجِع
feminine	*rēj3a*	راجْعة
plural	*rēj3īn*	راجْعين

عَيْلِةْ أبو ماضي رِجْعوا عَ بْعلْبك.

Abo Madi's family returned to Baalbek.

لمّا إرْجع عَ لِبْنان بدّي عيش بِالضَّيْعة.

When I go back to Lebanon, I will live in the village.

رِجِع يَعْمِل نفس المُشْكِلِة كِرْمال الكهْربا.

He went back to causing the same problem about the electricity.

ما بْتِـرجعي عالبيْت لْوَحْدِك؟

Don't you go back home alone?

إذا بدّك نِحْكي إنْكْليزي، عادي بِفْهم عليْك بسّ تعا نِرْجع للبْناني أحْسن.

If you want to talk in English, it's okay. I can understand you, but it's better if we go back to speaking Lebanese.

to ride رِكِب

	perfect		imperfect		bi-imperfect	
ána	*rkíbit*	رْكِبِت	*írkab*	إرْكَب	*bírkab*	بِركَب
níħna	*rkíbna*	رْكِبْنا	*nírkab*	نِرْكَب	*mnírkab*	مْنِـركَب
ínta	*rkíbit*	رْكِبْت	*tírkab*	تِرْكَب	*btírkab*	بْتِـركَب
ínti	*rkíbti*	رْكِبْتي	*tírkabi*	تِرْكَبي	*btírkabi*	بْتِـركَبي
íntu	*rkíbtu*	رْكِبْتوا	*tírkabu*	تِرْكَبوا	*btírkabu*	بْتِـركَبوا
húwwi	*ríkib*	رِكِب	*yírkab*	يِرْكَب	*byírkab*	بْيِـركَب
híyyi	*ríkbit*	رِكْبِت	*tírkab*	تِرْكَب	*btírkab*	بْتِـركَب
hínni	*ríkbu*	رِكْبوا	*yírkabu*	يِرْكَبوا	*byírkabu*	بْيِـركَبوا

	imperative	
ínta	*rkāb*	رْكاب
ínti	*rkábi*	رْكَبي
íntu	*rkábu*	رْكَبوا

	active participle	
masculine	*rēkib*	راكِب
feminine	*rēkbi*	راكْبِة
plural	*rēkbīn*	راكْبين

أخدِت الأَوْلاد عَ مدينِةِ الملاهي ورِكْبوا بِالتّرِيْن المجْنون ونْبسطوا فيه.

I took the kids to the amusement park, and they enjoyed riding the roller coaster.

عم إرْكب سِيّارة مرْسيدِس موْديْل الـ٢٠٠٠.

I'm driving a Mercedes model 2000.

كِلّ يوْم ميرا بْتِـركب بِالباص عالسّاعة ٨ الصُّبُح.

Every day Mira takes the bus at 8 a.m.

إسْمعْني ساري ما تِرْكب بالباص لأنّو بطيء.
كرْمال توصل بكّير، فيك تِرْكب بِالفان أَوْ بِالتّاكْسي.

Listen to me, Sari, don't ride the bus because it's slow.
To get there early, you can take a van or taxi.

شو لوَيْن رايْحة! رْكبي معي، بْوَصّْلِك.

Hey, where are you going? Come with me; I'll take you.

to throw رَمى

	perfect		imperfect		bi-imperfect	
ána	*ramēt*	رَميْت	*írmi*	إرْمي	*bírmi*	بِرْمي
níḫna	*ramáyna*	رَمَيْنا	*nírmi*	نِرْمي	*mnírmi*	مْنِـرمي
ínta	*ramēt*	رَميْت	*tírmi*	تِرْمي	*btírmi*	بْتِـرمي
ínti	*ramáyti*	رَمَيْتي	*tírmi*	تِرْمي	*btírmi*	بْتِـرمي
íntu	*ramáytu*	رَمَيْتوا	*tírmu*	تِرْموا	*btírmu*	بْتِـرموا
húwwi	*ráma*	رَمى	*yírmi*	يِرْمي	*byírmi*	بْيِـرمي
híyyi	*rámit*	رَمِت	*tírmi*	تِرْمي	*btírmi*	بْتِـرمي
hínni	*rámu*	رَموا	*yírmu*	يِرْموا	*byírmu*	بْيِـرموا

	imperative	
ínta	*rmī*	رْمي
ínti	*rmī*	رْمي
íntu	*rmū*	رْموا

	active participle	
masculine	*rēmi*	رامي
feminine	*rēmyi*	رامْية
plural	*rēmyīn*	رامْيين

رموا كْتير قناني عالطُّرُقات.

They threw a lot of bottles in the streets.

ما تِرْمي حْجار كِرْمال ما تِئْذي حدا.

Don't throw stones so that no one gets hurt.

ليْه بْتِـرمي يوْم الأحد زْبالِة؟ بْتعْرِف إنّو سوكْلين ما بْيِجوا هاليوْم!

Why do you throw out garbage on Sundays? You know the garbage collectors don't come on that day!

رْمي هْمومك وَراك.

Throw your worries behind you.

هالمنْجرة رامْيين كْتير ألْواح خشب عالطّريق.

This carpentry shop has thrown a lot of wood onto the road.

40 *hollow measure I* **to visit** زار

	perfect		imperfect		bi-imperfect	
ána	*zírit*	زِرِت	*zūr*	زور	*bzūr*	بْزور
níħna	*zírna*	زِرْنا	*nzūr*	نْزور	*minzūr*	مِنْزور
ínta	*zírit*	زِرِت	*tzūr*	تْزور	*bitzūr*	بِتْزور
ínti	*zírti*	زِرْتي	*tzūri*	تْزوري	*bitzūri*	بِتْزوري
íntu	*zírtu*	زِرْتوا	*tzūru*	تْزوروا	*bitzūru*	بِتْزوروا
húwwi	*zār*	زار	*yzūr*	يْزور	*bizūr*	بيزور
híyyi	*zārit*	زارِت	*tzūr*	تْزور	*bitzūr*	بِتْزور
hínni	*zāru*	زاروا	*yzūru*	يْزوروا	*bizūru*	بيزوروا

	imperative	
ínta	*zūr*	زور
ínti	*zūri*	زوري
íntu	*zūru*	زوروا

	active participle	
masculine	*zēyir*	زايِر
feminine	*zēyra*	زايْرة
plural	*zēyrīn*	زايْرين

زِرْتوا أقارايْبينْكُن بِالعيد؟

Did you visit your relatives on the holiday?

بِدِّك تْزوري خيِّك بِالمِسْتَشْفى؟

Do you want to visit your brother in the hospital?

بِتْحِبّ تْزور جْبيْل كِلّ صَيْفية؟

Do you like to visit Byblos [Jubayl] every summer?

كِلّ سِنِة مِنْزور أقرايْبينّا لمّا نْقرِّر نِنْزِل عَ لِبْنان.

Every year, we visit our relatives when we decide to go back to Lebanon.

قرّروا يِنْزْلوا عَ صَيْدا كِرْمال يْزوروا قلْعِةْ صَيْدا البحْرية.

They decided to go to Sidon to visit Sidon's Sea Castle.

 sound measure III

to help

ساعَد

	perfect		imperfect		bi-imperfect	
ána	*sē3ádit*	ساعَدت	*sē3id*	ساعِد	*bsē3id*	بْساعِد
níħna	*sē3ádna*	ساعَدْنا	*nsē3id*	نْساعِد	*minsē3id*	مِنْساعِد
ínta	*sē3ádit*	ساعَدت	*tsē3id*	تْساعِد	*bitsē3id*	بِتْساعِد
ínti	*sē3ádti*	ساعَدْتي	*tsē3di*	تْساعْدي	*bitsē3di*	بِتْساعْدي
íntu	*sē3ádtu*	ساعَدْتوا	*tsē3du*	تْساعْدوا	*bitsē3du*	بِتْساعْدوا
húwwi	*sē3ad*	ساعَد	*ysē3id*	يْساعِد	*bisē3id*	بيساعِد
híyyi	*sē3adit*	ساعَدِت	*tsē3id*	تْساعِد	*bitsē3id*	بِتْساعِد
hínni	*sē3adu*	ساعَدوا	*ysē3du*	يْساعْدوا	*bisē3du*	بيساعْدوا

	imperative	
ínta	*sē3id*	ساعِد
ínti	*sē3di*	ساعْدي
íntu	*sē3du*	ساعْدوا

	active participle	
masculine	*msē3id*	مْساعِد
feminine	*msē3di*	مْساعْدِة
plural	*msē3dīn*	مْساعْدين

جوْرْج بيساعِد عَيْلْتو.
George helps his family.

فيني ساعِد؟
May I help you?

فِيْن الجّيران يْساعْدوا لَيزْرَعوا الحَيّ؟
Can the neighbors help in planting the neighborhood?

روحي جُويل، ساعْدي بَيِّك بِالمَكْتَب.
Joelle, go help your father at the office.

مِس، لَيْش ما بِقْدر ساعِد رِفْقاتي بِالاِمْتِحان؟
Teacher, why can't I help my friends during the exam?

ما ساعدْتوا لجِدّك بِالإغْراض؟
Didn't you help your grandfather with his bags?

	perfect		imperfect		bi-imperfect	
ána	*saʔálit*	سَأَلِت	*ísʔal*	إِسْأَل	*bísʔal*	بِسْأَل
níђna	*saʔálna*	سَأَلْنا	*nísʔal*	نِسْأَل	*mnísʔal*	مْنِسْأَل
ínta	*saʔálit*	سَأَلِت	*tísʔal*	تِسْأَل	*btísʔal*	بْتِسْأَل
ínti	*saʔálti*	سَأَلْتي	*tísʔali*	تِسْأَلي	*btísʔali*	بْتِسْأَلي
íntu	*saʔáltu*	سَأَلْتوا	*tísʔalu*	تِسْأَلوا	*btísʔalu*	بْتِسْأَلوا
húwwi	*sáʔal*	سَأَل	*yísʔal*	يِسْأَل	*byísʔal*	بْيِسْأَل
híyyi	*sáʔalit*	سَأَلِت	*tísʔal*	تِسْأَل	*btísʔal*	بْتِسْأَل
hínni	*sáʔalu*	سَأَلوا	*yísʔalu*	يِسْأَلوا	*byísʔalu*	بْيِسْأَلوا

	imperative	
ínta	*sʔāl*	سْآل
ínti	*sʔáli*	سْأَلي
íntu	*sʔálu*	سْأَلوا

	active participle	
masculine	*sēʔil*	سائِل
feminine	*sēʔli*	سائْلة
plural	*sēʔlīn*	سائْلين

لمى عم تِسْأل إذا في جِبْنِة بِيْكون عِنْدْكُن بِالمحلّ.
Lama is asking if there is Picon cheese in your shop.

سألِت عنّك بِالنّادي.
I asked about you at the gym.

ما بْتِسْألوا الإسْتاذ عن المادّة. ليْش؟
You never ask the teacher about the subject. Why?

سْآل الحاج أبو خالِد اِللي قاعِد بِالقهْوِة عن الطّريق.
رح يْدِلّك لأنّو زلْمِة قديم بِالمنْطقة، بِيَعْرِفا كِلّا.
Ask Haj Abo Khaled, the one sitting in the coffee shop, for directions. He will show you because he's been in the area for a long time and knows it well.

الصّحفية سائْلِة عن البْروفيسور الجّامْعي لتعْمِل معو مُقابلِة عالتِّلِفزْيوْن.
The journalist has asked about the university professor in order to conduct a television interview with him.

43 *sound measure X* **to use** سْتَعْمَل

	perfect		imperfect		bi-imperfect	
ána	*sta3málit*	سْتَعْمَلت	*istá3mil*	إسْتَعْمِل	*bistá3mil*	بِسْتَعْمِل
níħna	*sta3málna*	سْتَعْمَلْنا	*nistá3mil*	نِسْتَعْمِل	*mnistá3mil*	مْنِسْتَعْمِل
ínta	*sta3málit*	سْتَعْمَلت	*tistá3mil*	تِسْتَعْمِل	*btistá3mil*	بْتِسْتَعْمِل
ínti	*sta3málti*	سْتَعْمَلْتي	*tistá3mli*	تِسْتَعْمْلي	*btistá3mli*	بْتِسْتَعْمْلي
íntu	*sta3máltu*	سْتَعْمَلْتوا	*tistá3mlu*	تِسْتَعْمْلوا	*btistá3mlu*	بْتِسْتَعْمْلوا
húwwi	*stá3mal*	سْتَعْمَل	*yistá3mil*	يِسْتَعْمِل	*byistá3mil*	بْيِسْتَعْمِل
híyyi	*stá3malit*	سْتَعْمَلت	*tistá3mil*	تِسْتَعْمِل	*btistá3mil*	بْتِسْتَعْمِل
hínni	*stá3malu*	سْتَعْمَلوا	*yistá3mlu*	يِسْتَعْمْلوا	*byistá3mlu*	بْيِسْتَعْمْلوا

	imperative	
ínta	*stá3mil*	سْتَعْمِل
ínti	*stá3mli*	سْتَعْمْلي
íntu	*stá3mlu*	سْتَعْمْلوا

	active participle	
masculine	*mistá3mil*	مِسْتَعْمِل
feminine	*mistá3mli*	مِسْتَعْمْلِة
plural	*mista3mlīn*	مِسْتَعْمْلين

كِلُّن سْتعْملوا الأصونْصير، إلاّ أنا طْلِعِت عالدّرج.

Everyone used the elevator except me. I took the stairs.

مالِك بْيِسْتعْمِل عضلاتو تَيحْمُل الغْراض.

Malik uses his muscles to carry the bags.

واو، عم تِسْتعْمْلي مُبيِّض للبشرة؟

Wow, are you using skin whitening cream?

ما بِسْتعْمِل ماكينِة حْلاقة لأنّا بْتوجِّع.

I don't use an electric razor because it hurts.

سْتعْمْلوا هالبِـرنامِج، بينظِّمْلْكُن وَقتْكُن.

Use this program. It organizes your time.

سْتعْمِل عقْلك وفكِّر بِالمَوْضوع.

Use your mind and think about the subject.

irregular measure X

to enjoy ستْهَنّى

	perfect		imperfect		bi-imperfect	
ána	*sthannēt*	ستْهَنّيْت	*isthánna*	إسْتْهَنّى	*bisthánna*	بِستْهَنّى
níħna	*sthannáyna*	ستْهَنّيْنا	*nisthánna*	نِستْهَنّى	*mnisthánna*	مْنِستْهَنّى
ínta	*sthannēt*	ستْهَنّيْت	*tisthánna*	تِستْهَنّى	*btisthánna*	بْتِستْهَنّى
ínti	*sthannáyti*	ستْهَنّيْتي	*tisthánni*	تِستْهَنّي	*btisthánni*	بْتِستْهَنّي
íntu	*sthannáytu*	ستْهَنّيْتوا	*tisthánnu*	تِستْهَنّوا	*btisthánnu*	بْتِستْهَنّوا
húwwi	*sthánna*	ستْهَنّى	*yisthánna*	يِستْهَنّى	*byisthánna*	بْيِستْهَنّى
híyyi	*sthánnit*	ستْهَنِّت	*tisthánna*	تِستْهَنّى	*btisthánna*	بْتِستْهَنّى
hínni	*sthánnu*	ستْهَنّوا	*yisthánnu*	يِستْهَنّوا	*byisthánnu*	بْيِستْهَنّوا

	imperative	
ínta	*sthánna*	ستْهَنّى
ínti	*sthánni*	ستْهَنّي
íntu	*sthánnu*	ستْهَنّوا

	active participle	
masculine	*misthánni*	مِستْهَنّي
feminine	*misthanníyyi*	مِستْهَنِّيّة
plural	*misthannyīn*	مِستْهَنْيين

ستْهَنّيْتي بْحفْلِة مْبارِح؟
Did you have fun at the party last night?

خلّيني إسْتْهَنّى بْأكْلي.
Let me enjoy my food.

نْشالْله بْيِستْهَنّى بِالشّغِل الجْديد.
I hope he enjoys his new job.

مِش مِستْهَنّي بْأيّ شي بْحَياتو.
He's not satisfied with anything in his life.

مِستْهَنْيين بِالسِّيّارة الجْديدِة.
They're enjoying the new car.

sound measure II

to close

سَكَّر

	perfect		imperfect		bi-imperfect	
ána	*sakkárit*	سَكَّرِت	*sákkir*	سَكِّر	*bsákkir*	بْسَكِّر
níḫna	*sakkárna*	سَكَّرْنا	*nsákkir*	نْسَكِّر	*minsákkir*	مِنْسَكِّر
ínta	*sakkárit*	سَكَّرِت	*tsákkir*	تْسَكِّر	*bitsákkir*	بِتْسَكِّر
ínti	*sakkárti*	سَكَّرْتي	*tsákkri*	تْسَكّْري	*bitsákkri*	بِتْسَكّْري
íntu	*sakkártu*	سَكَّرْتوا	*tsákkru*	تْسَكّْروا	*bitsákkru*	بِتْسَكّْروا
húwwi	*sákkar*	سَكَّر	*ysákkir*	يْسَكِّر	*bisákkir*	بيسَكِّر
híyyi	*sákkarit*	سَكَّرِت	*tsákkir*	تْسَكِّر	*bitsákkir*	بِتْسَكِّر
hínni	*sákkaru*	سَكَّروا	*ysákkru*	يْسَكّْروا	*bisákkru*	بيسَكّْروا

	imperative	
ínta	*sákkir*	سَكِّر
ínti	*sákkri*	سَكّْري
íntu	*sákkru*	سَكّْروا

	active participle	
masculine	*msákkir*	مْسَكِّر
feminine	*msákkra*	مْسَكّْرَة
plural	*msakkrīn*	مْسَكّْرين

حسن سكّر صفْحاتو عالإنْتِرنت.

Hassan deleted his accounts [pages] on the Internet.

كِلّ يوْم مِنْسكِّر المطْعم عالسّاعة ١٢ بِاللّيْل.

We close the restaurant at midnight every day.

أيوب بيسكِّر الصَّنْدوق مْنيح.

Ayoub closes the box very well.

الجّارة منّا مْسكّْرة خزّان الماي اللي عالسّطِح.

The neighbor has not closed the water tank on the roof.

سكِّر الباب وَراك.

Shut the door behind you.

to live سَكَن

	perfect		imperfect		bi-imperfect	
ána	sakánit	سَكَنِت	ískun	إِسْكُن	bískun	بِسْكُن
níħna	sakánna	سَكَنّا	*nískun*	نِسْكُن	mnískun	مْنِسْكُن
ínta	sakánit	سَكَنِت	tískun	تِسْكُن	btískun	بْتِسْكُن
ínti	sakánti	سَكَنْتي	tískni	تِسْكْني	btískni	بْتِسْكْني
íntu	sakántu	سَكَنْتوا	tísknu	تِسْكْنوا	btísknu	بْتِسْكْنوا
húwwi	sákan	سَكَن	yískun	يِسْكُن	byískun	بْيِسْكُن
híyyi	sákanit	سَكَنِت	tískun	تِسْكُن	btískun	بْتِسْكُن
hínni	sákanu	سَكَنوا	yísknu	يِسْكْنوا	byísknu	بْيِسْكْنوا

	imperative	
ínta	skūn	سْكون
ínti	skíni	سْكِني
íntu	skínu	سْكِنوا

	active participle	
masculine	sēkin	ساكِن
feminine	sēkni	ساكْنِة
plural	sēknīn	ساكْنين

بيْت عمّي سكنوا حدّنا بِالضّيْعة.
My uncle and his family lived next to us in the village.

بدّي إسْكُن لَوَحْدي بِالجميْزِة.
I want to live alone in Gemayzeh.

شادي، ليْش ما بْتِسْكُن بْبيْت صْغير؟
Shadi, why don't you live in a small house?

مع مين ساكْنِة بِالبيْت؟
Who do you live with?

عَيْلتيْن ساكْنين سَوا بْنفْس الشّقّة.
Two families are living together in the same apartment.

sound measure I

to hear سِمِع

	perfect		imperfect		bi-imperfect	
ána	*smí3it*	سْمِعِت	*ísma3*	إسْمَع	*bísma3*	بِسْمَع
níђna	*smí3na*	سْمِعْنا	*nísma3*	نِسْمَع	*mnísma3*	مْنِسْمَع
ínta	*smí3it*	سْمِعِت	*tísma3*	تِسْمَع	*btísma3*	بْتِسْمَع
ínti	*smí3ti*	سْمِعْتي	*tísma3i*	تِسْمَعي	*btísma3i*	بْتِسْمَعي
íntu	*smí3tu*	سْمِعْتوا	*tísma3u*	تِسْمَعوا	*btísma3u*	بْتِسْمَعوا
húwwi	*sími3*	سِمِع	*yísma3*	يِسْمَع	*byísma3*	بْيِسْمَع
híyyi	*sím3it*	سِمْعِت	*tísma3*	تِسْمَع	*btísma3*	بْتِسْمَع
hínni	*sím3u*	سِمْعوا	*yísma3u*	يِسْمَعوا	*byísma3u*	بْيِسْمَعوا

	imperative	
ínta	*smā3*	سْماع
ínti	*smá3i*	سْمَعي
íntu	*smá3u*	سْمَعوا

	active participle	
masculine	*sēmi3*	سامِع
feminine	*sēm3a*	سامْعة
plural	*sēm3īn*	سامْعين

سْمِعْنا رح تِشْتِـروا غِرْفِة نوْم جْديدِة.

We heard that you will buy a new bedroom.

ما بْشوفِك غيْر قاعْدِة تِسْمعي لفيْروز عالصُّبْح.

I always see you listening to Fayrouz in the morning.

بْحِبّ إسْمع للمذيع ساري الخليلي كِلّ يوْم عَ راديْو سَوا.

I love listening to the broadcaster Sari Alkhalili every day on Radio Sawa.

العالم عم يِسْمعوا مُباشر لمجْلِس الوُزرا مع إنّو عارْفين النّتيجِة.

Everyone is listening live to the Council of Ministers,
although they already know the results.

سْمعوا كلام أهاليكُن وما تِطْلعوا لَوَحْدْكُن بِاللّيْل.

Listen to your parents and don't go out alone at night.

	perfect		imperfect		bi-imperfect	
ána	*šífit*	شِفِت	*šūf*	شوف	*bšūf*	بْشوف
níḫna	*šífna*	شِفْنا	*nšūf*	نْشوف	*minšūf*	مِنْشوف
ínta	*šífit*	شِفِت	*tšūf*	تْشوف	*bitšūf*	بِتْشوف
ínti	*šífti*	شِفْتي	*tšūfi*	تْشوفي	*bitšūfi*	بِتْشوفي
íntu	*šíftu*	شِفْتوا	*tšūfu*	تْشوفوا	*bitšūfu*	بِتْشوفوا
húwwi	*šēf*	شاف	*yšūf*	يْشوف	*bišūf*	بيشوف
híyyi	*šēfit*	شافِت	*tšūf*	تْشوف	*bitšūf*	بِتْشوف
hínni	*šēfu*	شافوا	*yšūfu*	يْشوفوا	*bišūfu*	بيشوفوا

	imperative	
ínta	*šūf*	شوف
ínti	*šūfi*	شوفي
íntu	*šūfu*	شوفو

	active participle	
masculine	*šēyif*	شايِف
feminine	*šēyfi*	شايْفِة
plural	*šēyfīn*	شايْفين

ما شِفْنا هِشام مْبارِح.

We didn't see Hisham yesterday.

بِدّو يْشوف مِن ويْن يْجيب دعِم لنشِر رِوايْتو.

He wants to see where he can get the funds to publish his novel.

أيمْتى بدْكُن تْشوفوا الشِّقّة الجْديدِة؟

When do you want to see the new apartment?

بُكْرا بْشوف إذا فيِّ روح ع حفْلِة فيرْوز بمْهرجانات بيْت الدّين.

Tomorrow, I'll see if I'm going to go to a Fayrouz concert at the Beit Ed-Dine festival.

شوفي هالفِسْتان وعْطيني رأْيِك.

Look at this dress and give me your opinion.

 defective measure VIII

to buy

شْتَرى

	perfect		imperfect		bi-imperfect	
ána	*štarēt*	شْتَرَيْت	*íštri*	إشْتْـري	*bíštri*	بِشْتْـري
níḥna	*štaráyna*	شْتَرَيْنا	*níštri*	نِشْتْـري	*mníštri*	مْنِشْتْـري
ínta	*štarēt*	شْتَرَيْت	*tíštri*	تِشْتْري	*btíštri*	بْتِشْتْري
ínti	*štaráyti*	شْتَرَيْتي	*tíštri*	تِشْتْري	*btíštri*	بْتِشْتْري
íntu	*štaráytu*	شْتَرَيْتوا	*tíštru*	تِشْتْروا	*btíštru*	بْتِشْتْروا
húwwi	*štára*	شْتَرى	*yíštri*	يِشْتْري	*byíštri*	بْيِشْتْري
híyyi	*štárit*	شْتَرِت	*tíštri*	تِشْتْري	*btíštri*	بْتِشْتْري
hínni	*štáru*	شْتَروا	*yíštru*	يِشْتْروا	*byíštru*	بْيِشْتْروا

	imperative	
ínta	*štíri*	شْتِـري
ínti	*štíri*	شْتِـري
íntu	*štíru*	شْتِـروا

	active participle	
masculine	*míštri*	مِشْتْـري
feminine	*mištríyyi*	مِشْتْـرِيّة
plural	*mištriyyīn*	مِشْتْـرِيّين

لَيْه بدّك تِشْتْـري سِيّارة جْديدِة؟

Why do you want to buy a new car?

ما شْتَرَيْت شي بِالسّوق.

I didn't buy anything at the market.

شْتِـري هلّق قبِل ما يِطْلع سِعْرو بعْدَيْن.

Buy it now before its price goes up later.

هُوِّ كِلّ سِنِة أَوْ سِنْتين بْيِشْتْـري موْبايْل جْديد.

He buys a new mobile phone every year or two.

علي عم يْجمِّع مصرِيّاتو لَيِشْتْـري بيْت.

Ali is saving his money to buy a house.

50 *sound measure VIII* to work شْتَغَل

	perfect		imperfect		bi-imperfect	
ána	*štaɣálit*	شْتَغَلت	*íštiɣil*	إشْتِغِل	*bíštiɣil*	بِشْتِغِل
níђna	*štaɣálna*	شْتَغَلْنا	*níštiɣil*	نِشْتِغِل	*mníštiɣil*	مْنِشْتِغِل
ínta	*štaɣálit*	شْتَغَلت	*tíštiɣil*	تِشْتِغِل	*btíštiɣil*	بْتِشْتِغِل
ínti	*štaɣálti*	شْتَغَلْتي	*tištíɣli*	تِشْتِغْلي	*btištíɣli*	بْتِشْتِغْلي
íntu	*štaɣáltu*	شْتَغَلْتوا	*tištíɣlu*	تِشْتِغْلوا	*btištíɣlu*	بْتِشْتِغْلوا
húwwi	*štáɣal*	شْتَغَل	*yíštiɣil*	يِشْتِغِل	*byístiɣil*	بْيِشْتِغِل
híyyi	*štáɣalit*	شْتَغَلت	*tíštiɣil*	تِشْتِغِل	*btíštiɣil*	بْتِشْتِغِل
hínni	*štáɣalu*	شْتَغَلوا	*yištíɣlu*	يِشْتِغْلوا	*byištíɣlu*	بْيِشْتِغْلوا

	imperative	
ínta	*štíɣil*	شْتِغِل
ínti	*štíɣli*	شْتِغْلي
íntu	*štíɣlu*	شْتِغْلوا

	active participle	
masculine	*mištíɣil*	مِشْتِغِل
feminine	*mištíɣli*	مِشْتِغْلة
plural	*mištiɣlīn*	مِشْتِغْلين

وين شْتغلِت؟

Where did you work?

كِنْت إشْتِغِل بْهاي الشّرْكِة ١٠ سْنين.

I've worked at this company for 10 years.

اليوْم رح يِشْتِغِل بِالبيْت.

He'll work at home today.

بِتْحِبّ تِشْتِغِل دُكْتوْرة.

She loves to work as a doctor.

أبداً ما مْنِشْتِغِل بْعُطْلِتْنا الأُسْبوعية.

We never work during the weekend.

بِشْتِغِل عنْد نجّار.

I work at Najjar [coffee shop].

sound measure I

to drink

شِرِب

	perfect		imperfect		bi-imperfect	
ána	*šribít*	شْرِبِت	*íšrab*	إِشْرَب	*bíšrab*	بِشْرَب
níḫna	*šríbna*	شْرِبْنا	*níšrab*	نِشْرَب	*mníšrab*	مْنِشْرَب
ínta	*šribít*	شْرِبِت	*tíšrab*	تِشْرَب	*btíšrab*	بْتِشْرَب
ínti	*šríbti*	شْرِبْتي	*tíšrabi*	تِشْرَبي	*btíšrabi*	بْتِشْرَبي
íntu	*šríbtu*	شْرِبْتوا	*tíšrabu*	تِشْرَبوا	*btíšrabu*	بْتِشْرَبوا
húwwi	*šírib*	شِرِب	*yíšrab*	يِشْرَب	*byíšrab*	بْيِشْرَب
híyyi	*šírbit*	شِرْبِت	*tíšrab*	تِشْرَب	*btíšrab*	بْتِشْرَب
hínni	*šírbu*	شِرْبوا	*yíšrabu*	يِشْرَبوا	*byíšrabu*	بْيِشْرَبوا

	imperative	
ínta	*šrāb*	شْراب
ínti	*šrábi*	شْرَبي
íntu	*šrábu*	شْرَبوا

	active participle	
masculine	*šērib*	شارِب
feminine	*šērbi*	شارْبِة
plural	*šērbīn*	شارْبين

عَم تِشْرب قهْوِة.

She is drinking coffee.

ما بْحَياتُن شارْبين كوحول.

They have never drunk alcohol.

شِرْبِت تْلات كاسات شاي هَيْدا الصُّبُح.

She drank three cups of tea this morning.

شْرَبي هَيْدا، رَح تْصيري مْنيحَة.

Drink this. You'll feel better.

بْيِشْرَب عِلْبِة دِخّان بِاليوْم.

He smokes a pack of cigarettes a day.

	perfect		imperfect		bi-imperfect	
ána	*šakárit*	شَكَرِت	*íškur*	إِشْكُر	*bíškur*	بِشْكُر
níħna	*šakárna*	شَكَرْنا	*níškur*	نِشْكُر	*mníškur*	مْنِشْكُر
ínta	*šakárit*	شَكَرِت	*tíškur*	تِشْكُر	*btíškur*	بْتِشْكُر
ínti	*šakárti*	شَكَرْتي	*tíškri*	تِشْكْري	*btíškri*	بْتِشْكْري
íntu	*šakártu*	شَكَرْتوا	*tíškru*	تِشْكْروا	*btíškru*	بْتِشْكْروا
húwwi	*šákar*	شَكَر	*yíškur*	يِشْكُر	*byíškur*	بْيِشْكُر
híyyi	*šákarit*	شَكَرِت	*tíškur*	تِشْكُر	*btíškur*	بْتِشْكُر
hínni	*šákaru*	شَكَروا	*yíškru*	يِشْكْروا	*byíškru*	بْيِشْكْروا

	imperative	
ínta	*škūr*	شْكور
ínti	*škíri*	شْكِري
íntu	*škíru*	شْكِروا

	active participle	
masculine	*šēkir*	شاكِر
feminine	*šēkra*	شاكْرَة
plural	*šēkrīn*	شاكْرين

شكرِت شِرْكِةْ الاتِّصالات الزّبائِن على اِسْتِخْدام خدماتا الجْديدِة.

The telecommunication company thanked its customers for using its new services.

بِشْكُر الحُضور على مشارِكِتْن بِافْتِتاح العرْض المسْرحي الجْديد بمِسْرح دوّار الشّمِس.

I thank the audience for their participation in the premiere of the new show in Sunflower theater.

سلْمى كتبِت كْتاب بْتِشْكُر فيه الدُّكْتور أَنْطْوان.

Salma wrote a book in which she thanked Dr. Antoine.

ليه ما بْتِشْكُر أهْلك اِللى وِقْفوا حدّك كِلّ الطّريق؟

Why don't you thank your parents who stood by your side throughout your journey?

شْكور ربّك على كِلّ شي!

Thank God for everything!

53 *hollow measure I* **to become** صار

	perfect		imperfect		bi-imperfect	
ána	*ṣīrit*	صِرت	*ṣīr*	صير	*bṣīr*	بْصير
níḫna	*ṣírna*	صِرْنا	*nṣīr*	نْصير	*minṣīr*	مِنْصير
ínta	*ṣírit*	صِرت	*tṣīr*	تْصير	*bitṣīr*	بِتْصير
ínti	*ṣírti*	صِرْتي	*tṣīri*	تْصيري	*bitṣīri*	بِتْصيري
íntu	*ṣírtu*	صِرْتوا	*tṣīru*	تْصيروا	*bitṣīru*	بِتْصيروا
húwwi	*ṣār*	صار	*yṣīr*	يْصير	*biṣīr*	بيصير
híyyi	*ṣārit*	صارِت	*tṣīr*	تْصير	*bitṣīr*	بِتْصير
hínni	*ṣāru*	صاروا	*yṣīru*	يْصيروا	*biṣīru*	بيصيروا

	imperative	
ínta	*ṣīr*	صير
ínti	*ṣīri*	صيري
íntu	*ṣīru*	صيروا

	active participle	
masculine	*ṣāyir*	صايِر
feminine	*ṣāyra*	صايْرة
plural	*ṣāyrīn*	صايْرين

كيف صِرت؟

How are you feeling now?

بسّ تْصير تِفْهم رْجاع حْكي معي.

When you become wise enough, come back and talk to me.

لمّا صير مُدير رح غيِّر كْتير أشْيا.

When I become manager, I will change a lot of things.

هالحكيْ ما بيصير بِالتِّلِفوْن.

This conversation should not take place over the telephone.

صايِر كْتير زِنِخ.

He's become very silly.

	perfect		imperfect		bi-imperfect	
ána	*dĥíkit*	ضْحِكِت	*ídĥak*	إِضْحَك	*bídĥak*	بِضْحَك
níĥna	*dĥíkna*	ضْحِكْنا	*nídĥak*	نِضْحَك	*mnídĥak*	مْنِضْحَك
ínta	*dĥíkit*	ضْحِكِت	*tídĥak*	تِضْحَك	*btídĥak*	بْتِضْحَك
ínti	*dĥíkti*	ضْحِكْتي	*tídĥaki*	تِضْحَكي	*btídĥaki*	بْتِضْحَكي
íntu	*dĥíktu*	ضْحِكْتوا	*tídĥaku*	تِضْحَكوا	*btídĥaku*	بْتِضْحَكوا
húwwi	*díĥik*	ضِحِك	*yídĥak*	يِضْحَك	*byídĥak*	بْيِضْحَك
híyyi	*díĥkit*	ضِحْكِت	*tídĥak*	تِضْحَك	*btídĥak*	بْتِضْحَك
hínni	*díĥku*	ضِحْكوا	*yídĥak*	يِضْحَكوا	*byídĥak*	بْيِضْحَكوا

	imperative	
ínta	*dĥāk*	ضْحاك
ínti	*dĥáki*	ضْحَكي
íntu	*dĥáku*	ضْحَكوا

	active participle	
masculine	*dēĥik*	ضاحِك
feminine	*dēĥki*	ضاحْكِة
plural	*dēĥkīn*	ضاحْكين

سِتّي ضِحْكِت مِن قلْبا.

My grandmother laughed wholeheartedly.

عبّاس بْيِحْكي نُكْتِة بايْخة وبْيِضْحك عليا.

Abbas tells a silly joke and laughs at it.

ليْه ما بْتِضْحكوا وبْتِنْبُسْطوا، حاجِة قالْبينْلي إياها نِكِد.

Why don’t you laugh and enjoy yourselves instead of being grumpy?

بِضْحك كْتير بس إتْفرّج ع ميسْترِ بين.

I laugh alot when I watch Mr Bean.

ضاحِك عليْكُن بيّاع التِّلِفوْنات.

The phone seller has deceived you.

55 *geminate measure I* **to stay** ضَلّ

	perfect		imperfect		bi-imperfect	
ána	*ḍallēt*	ضَلّيْت	*ḍall*	ضَلّ	*bḍall*	بْضَلّ
níħna	*ḍalláyna*	ضَلَّيْنا	*nḍall*	نْضَلّ	*minḍáll*	مِنْضَلّ
ínta	*ḍallēt*	ضَلّيْت	*tḍall*	تْضَلّ	*bitḍáll*	بِتْضَلّ
ínti	*ḍalláyti*	ضَلَّيْتي	*tḍálli*	تْضَلّي	*bitḍálli*	بِتْضَلّي
íntu	*ḍalláytu*	ضَلَّيْتوا	*tḍállu*	تْضَلّوا	*bitḍállu*	بِتْضَلّوا
húwwi	*ḍall*	ضَلّ	*yḍall*	يْضَلّ	*biḍáll*	بيضَلّ
híyyi	*ḍállit*	ضَلِّت	*tḍall*	تْضَلّ	*bitḍáll*	بِتْضَلّ
hínni	*ḍállu*	ضَلّوا	*yḍállu*	يْضَلّوا	*biḍállu*	بيضَلّوا

	imperative	
ínta	*ḍall*	ضَلّ
ínti	*ḍálli*	ضَلّي
íntu	*ḍállu*	ضَلّوا

active participle		
masculine	*ḍālil*	ضالِل
feminine	*ḍālli*	ضالّة
plural	*ḍāllīn*	ضالّين

ضلَّيْتوا أُسْبوع بْحِمّانا؟

Did you stay in Hamana for one week?

ليْه بِتْضلّي تْدِقّي عالباب؟

Why do you keep knocking on the door?

كِلّ مرّة بْضلّ ناطِرْكُن وما حدا بْيِجي لعِنْدي.

Every time I keep waiting for you guys, but no one shows up.

مِش ضالِل غيْر جوْرْج يَعْطينا رأْيو.

Only George has yet to give us his opinion.

ضلّي صلّي.

Keep praying!

ما تْضلّوا بِالشّارِع للمسا.

Don't stay out late.

56 *sound measure I* to cook طَبَخ

	perfect		imperfect		bi-imperfect	
ána	*ţabáxit*	طَبَخِت	*úţbux*	أُطْبُخ	*búţbux*	بُطْبُخ
níħna	*ţabáxna*	طَبَخْنا	*núţbux*	نُطْبُخ	*mnúţbux*	مْنُطْبُخ
ínta	*ţabáxit*	طَبَخِت	*túţbux*	تُطْبُخ	*btúţbux*	بْتُطْبُخ
ínti	*ţabáxti*	طَبَخْتي	*túţbxi*	تُطْبْخي	*btúţbxi*	بْتُطْبْخي
íntu	*ţabáxtu*	طَبَخْتوا	*túţbxu*	تُطْبْخوا	*btúţbxu*	بْتُطْبْخوا
húwwi	*ţábax*	طَبَخ	*yúţbux*	يُطْبُخ	*byúţbux*	بْيُطْبُخ
híyyi	*ţábaxit*	طَبَخِت	*túţbux*	تُطْبُخ	*btúţbux*	بْتُطْبُخ
hínni	*ţábaxu*	طَبَخوا	*yúţbxu*	يُطْبْخوا	*byúţbxu*	بْيُطْبْخوا

	imperative	
ínta	*ţbūx*	طْبوخ
ínti	*ţbúxi*	طْبُخي
íntu	*ţbúxu*	طْبُخوا

	active participle	
masculine	*ţābix*	طابِخ
feminine	*ţābxa*	طابْخَة
plural	*ţābxīn*	طابْخين

بْحِبّ أُطْبُخ بْمَطْبخ واسِع وكْبير.

I like to cook in a big, wide kitchen.

الماما طبختِ وَرَق عِنب مْبارِح.

My mom cooked stuffed vine leaves last night.

ما تْخلّيه يْقرّب عالمطْبخ. كِلّ ما يْيُطْبُخ طبْخة بْيِحْرِقا.

Don't let him go into the kitchen. Every time he cooks something, he burns it.

طْبُخوا حد الطّبْخة الرّئيسية مْقبِّلات كمان.

Prepare appetizers alongside the main dish.

بْتعْرِف إنّو بِالمطْبخ اللِّبْناني بْيُطْبْخوا ٤٤ صُنْف
بْتِنْحطّ عالطّاوْلِة قبْل الوَجْبِة الرّئيسية؟

Do you know that in Lebanese cuisine, they cook 44 kinds of the meze [side dishes] which they put on the table before they serve you the main dishes!

to request طَلَب

	perfect		imperfect		bi-imperfect	
ána	*ţalábit*	طَلَبِت	*íţlub*	إِطْلُب	*bíţlub*	بِطْلُب
níḫna	*ţalábna*	طَلَبْنا	*níţlub*	نِطْلُب	*mníţlub*	مْنِطْلُب
ínta	*ţalábit*	طَلَبِت	*tíţlub*	تِطْلُب	*btíţlub*	بْتِطْلُب
ínti	*ţalábti*	طَلَبْتي	*tíţilbi*	تِطِلْبي	*btíţilbi*	بْتِطِلْبي
íntu	*ţalábtu*	طَلَبْتوا	*tíţilbu*	تِطِلْبوا	*btíţilbu*	بْتِطِلْبوا
húwwi	*ţálab*	طَلَب	*yíţlub*	يِطْلُب	*byíţlub*	بْيِطْلُب
híyyi	*ţálabit*	طَلَبِت	*tíţlub*	تِطْلُب	*btíţlub*	بْتِطْلُب
hínni	*ţálabu*	طَلَبوا	*yíţilbu*	يِطِلْبوا	*byíţilbu*	بْيِطِلْبوا

	imperative	
ínta	*ţlūb*	طْلوب
ínti	*ţlúbi*	طْلُبي
íntu	*ţlúbu*	طْلُبوا

	active participle	
masculine	*ţālib*	طالِب
feminine	*ţālbi*	طالْبِة
plural	*ţālbīn*	طالْبين

طلبِت طلبية مِن عِنْد طحّان مع فاتورة مِن أُسْبوع.
I placed an order from Tahan by invoice a week ago.

ما فيكي تِطِلْبي بوفيْه مِن عِنْد طبْلية؟
Can't you order a buffet lunch from Tablieh?

ميرا بسّ تْروح عالجامْعة بْتِطْلُب تاكْسي.
Mira calls a taxi to get to college.

ما تِطْلُب مصاري لأنّو ما معي.
Don't ask [me] for money because I don't have any.

طْلُبوا بيتْزا عالغدا.
Order pizza for lunch.

58 *sound measure I* **to ascend** طِلِع

	perfect		imperfect		bi-imperfect	
ána	*ṭlí3it*	طْلِعِت	*íṭla3*	إطْلَع	*bíṭla3*	بطْلَع
níḫna	*ṭlí3na*	طْلِعْنا	*níṭla3*	نِطْلَع	*mníṭla3*	مْنِطْلَع
ínta	*ṭlí3it*	طْلِعِت	*tíṭla3*	تِطْلَع	*btíṭla3*	بْتِطْلَع
ínti	*ṭlí3ti*	طْلِعْتي	*tíṭla3i*	تِطْلَعي	*btíṭla3i*	بْتِطْلَعي
íntu	*ṭlí3tu*	طْلِعْتوا	*tíṭla3u*	تِطْلَعوا	*btíṭla3u*	بْتِطْلَعوا
húwwi	*ṭíli3*	طِلِع	*yíṭla3*	يِطْلَع	*byíṭla3*	بْيِطْلَع
híyyi	*ṭíl3it*	طِلْعِت	*tíṭla3*	تِطْلَع	*btíṭla3*	بْتِطْلَع
hínni	*ṭíl3u*	طِلْعوا	*yíṭla3u*	يِطْلَعوا	*byíṭla3u*	بْيِطْلَعوا

	imperative	
ínta	*ṭlā3*	طْلاع
ínti	*ṭlá3i*	طْلَعي
íntu	*ṭlá3u*	طْلَعوا

	active participle	
masculine	*ṭāli3*	طالِع
feminine	*ṭāl3a*	طالْعَة
plural	*ṭāl3īn*	طالْعين

مرْحبا سلْمى، بِتْحِبّي تِطْلعي معي عالحمْرا؟
Hi, Salma! Would you like to go with me to Hamra?

طْلِعِت جبِت شنْطْتي عن التّتْخيتي.
I went to get my bag from the attic.

أصْحاب رامي بْيِطْلعوا عَ فرَيا كِلّ أحد لَيتْزلّجوا.
Rami's friends go to Faraya every Sunday to ski.

أبو عُمر، طْلاع مِن السِّيّارة لَنِحْكي شْوَيّ.
Abo Omar, get out of the car to chat a bit.

مايا طالْعة بكّير عالمطار لتْلحِّق طِيّارتا.
Maya is going to the airport early to catch her plane.

طِلِع بِالفان مِنْشان يْروح عَ صور.
He got in the van to go to Tyre [Sour].

الشّمِس طِلْعِت وكْتير حِلْوِة.
The sun has risen, and it's beautiful.

sound measure I

to know

عِرِف

	perfect		imperfect		bi-imperfect	
ána	*3rífit*	عْرِفِت	*á3rif*	أَعْرِف	*bá3rif*	بَعْرِف
níħna	*3rífna*	عْرِفْنا	*ná3rif*	نَعْرِف	*mná3rif*	مْنَعْرِف
ínta	*3rífit*	عْرِفِت	*tá3rif*	تَعْرِف	*btá3rif*	بْتَعْرِف
ínti	*3rífti*	عْرِفْتي	*tá3rfi*	تَعْرْفي	*btá3rfi*	بْتَعْرْفي
íntu	*3ríftu*	عْرِفْتوا	*tá3rfu*	تَعْرْفوا	*btá3rfu*	بْتَعْرْفوا
húwwi	*3írif*	عِرِف	*yá3rif*	يَعْرِف	*byá3rif*	بْيَعْرِف
híyyi	*3írfit*	عِرْفِت	*tá3rif*	تَعْرِف	*btá3rif*	بْتَعْرِف
hínni	*3írfu*	عِرْفوا	*yá3rfu*	يَعْرْفوا	*byá3rfu*	بْيَعْرْفوا

	imperative	
ínta	*3rāf*	عْراف
ínti	*3ráfi*	عْرَفي
íntu	*3ráfu*	عْرَفوا

	active participle	
masculine	*3ērif*	عارِف
feminine	*3ērfi*	عارْفِة
plural	*3ērfīn*	عارْفين

⚠ Notice that the vowel of the imperfect prefix is ◌َ *a*. (This is also true for a couple of other verbs: ➲ **T-61** and **T-62**.)

عْرِفْتي إنّو رح يْجيبوا مُدير جْديد عالجّمْعية؟

Did you know that they will hire a new general manager for the organization?

بعْرِف غنّي أغاني للرّحْباني.

I know how to sing Rahbani songs.

بْتعْرْفوا إنّو الأعياد قرّبِت!

You know, the holidays are approaching!

مْنعْرِف إنْكُن قرّرْتوا ترْجعوا عَ لِبْنان.

We know that you decided to return to Lebanon.

ما بْتعْرِف كيف بيعمّروا بيْت!

You don't know how to build a house!

كِنت عارِف إنّي مريض السّبِت؟

Did you know that I was sick on Saturday?

نْشالْله أعْرِف حِلّ شي بْهالاِمْتِحان.

I hope that I'll answer something on that exam.

sound measure I

to invite عَزَم

	perfect		imperfect		bi-imperfect	
ána	*3azámit*	عَزَمِت	*í3zum*	إِعْزُم	*bí3zum*	بِعْزُم
níħna	*3azámna*	عَزَمْنا	*ní3zum*	نِعْزُم	*mní3zum*	مْنِعْزُم
ínta	*3azámit*	عَزَمِت	*tí3zum*	تِعْزُم	*btí3zum*	بْتِعْزُم
ínti	*3azámti*	عَزَمْتي	*tí3zmi*	تِعْزْمي	*btí3zmi*	بْتِعْزْمي
íntu	*3azámtu*	عَزَمْتوا	*tí3zmu*	تِعْزْموا	*btí3zmu*	بْتِعْزْموا
húwwi	*3ázam*	عَزَم	*yí3zum*	يِعْزُم	*byí3zum*	بْيِعْزُم
híyyi	*3ázamit*	عَزَمِت	*tí3zum*	تِعْزُم	*btí3zum*	بْتِعْزُم
hínni	*3ázamu*	عَزَموا	*yí3zmu*	يِعْزْموا	*byí3zmu*	بْيِعْزْموا

	imperative	
ínta	*3zūm*	عْزوم
ínti	*3zími*	عْزِمي
íntu	*3zímu*	عْزِموا

	active participle	
masculine	*3ēzim*	عازِم
feminine	*3ēzmi*	عازْمِة
plural	*3ēzmīn*	عازْمين

عزمْنا أصْحابْنا على العشا مْبارِح.

We invited our friends to dinner yesterday.

بْحِبّ إعْزم العالم على حفْلات الدّي جيْ اللى بِعْمِلا دايمْاً.

I like to invite people to the DJ parties I always have.

هالخِتْيار ما بْيِعْزم حدا لعِنْدو عالبيْت.

This old man doesn't invite anybody to his house.

عْزِمي صاحِبْتِك تْروح معْنا هَيْدا الأحد عالدّامور.

Invite your friend to go with us to the Damour river this Sunday.

عازْمين كْتير عالم على الحفْلِة.

They have invited a lot of people to the party.

to give عَطى

	perfect		imperfect		bi-imperfect	
ána	*3aṭēt*	عَطيْت	*ʔá3ṭi*	أَعْطي	*bá3ṭi*	بَعْطي
níḫna	*3aṭáyna*	عَطَيْنا	*ná3ṭi*	نَعْطي	*mná3ṭi*	مْنَعْطي
ínta	*3aṭēt*	عَطيت	*tá3ṭi*	تَعْطي	*btá3ṭi*	بْتَعْطي
ínti	*3aṭáyti*	عَطَيْتي	*tá3ṭi*	تَعْطي	*btá3ṭi*	بْتَعْطي
íntu	*3aṭáytu*	عَطَيْتوا	*tá3ṭu*	تَعْطوا	*btá3ṭu*	بْتَعْطوا
húwwi	*3áṭa*	عَطى	*yá3ṭi*	يَعْطي	*byá3ṭi*	بْيَعْطي
híyyi	*3áṭit*	عَطِت	*tá3ṭi*	تَعْطي	*btá3ṭi*	بْتَعْطي
hínni	*3áṭu*	عَطوا	*yá3ṭu*	يَعْطوا	*byá3ṭu*	بْيَعْطوا

	imperative	
ínta	*3ṭī*	عْطي
ínti	*3ṭī*	عْطي
íntu	*3ṭū*	عْطوا

	active participle	
masculine	*3āṭi*	عاطي
feminine	*3āṭyi*	عاطْيِة
plural	*3āṭyīn*	عاطْيين

⚠ Notice that the vowel of the imperfect prefix is َ *a*. (This is also true for a couple of other verbs: ➲ **T-59** and **T-62**.)

عطَيْت تالا شمِع؟

Did you give Tala candles?

بعْطي دْروس خُصوصية للطُّلاب الضُّعاف.

I give private lessons for weak students.

ما بْتعْطي حدا باسْوُرْد النِّت.

Don't give anybody the internet password.

عْطي رفيف كِبّايِة ماي.

Give Rafif a cup of water.

عاطْيِة مونة لِلفُقرا اللي بِالحيّ.

She has given food to the poor in the neighborhood.

62 *sound measure I* **to do** عِمِل

	perfect		imperfect		bi-imperfect	
ána	*3mílit*	عْمِلت	*á3mil*	أَعْمِل	*bá3mil*	بَعْمِل
níħna	*3mílna*	عْمِلْنا	*ná3mil*	نَعْمِل	*mná3mil*	مْنَعْمِل
ínta	*3mílit*	عْمِلت	*tá3mil*	تَعْمِل	*btá3mil*	بْتَعْمِل
ínti	*3mílti*	عْمِلْتي	*tá3mli*	تَعْمْلي	*btá3mli*	بْتَعْمْلي
íntu	*3míltu*	عْمِلْتوا	*tá3mlu*	تَعْمْلوا	*btá3mlu*	بْتَعْمْلوا
húwwi	*3ímil*	عِمِل	*yá3mil*	يَعْمِل	*byá3mil*	بْيَعْمِل
híyyi	*3ímlit*	عِمْلِت	*tá3mil*	تَعْمِل	*btá3mil*	بْتَعْمِل
hínni	*3ímlu*	عِمْلوا	*yá3mlu*	يَعْمْلوا	*byá3mlu*	بْيَعْمْلوا

	imperative	
ínta	*3mūl*	عْمول
ínti	*3míli*	عْمِلي
íntu	*3mílu*	عْمِلوا

	active participle	
masculine	*3āmil*	عامِل
feminine	*3āmli*	عامْلِة
plural	*3āmlīn*	عامْلين

⚠ Notice that the vowel of the imperfect prefix is َ *a*. (This is also true for a couple of other verbs: ➲ **T-59** and **T-61**.)

رح أعْمِل تبّولِة وصحِن بطاطا.
I will make tabbouleh and French fries.

شو عم تعْمِل؟
What are you doing?

شوفي كيف بعْمِل وتْعلّمي كِرْمال ما تعْمْلي غلط.
Watch how I make it and learn, so you won't do it wrong.

حازِم، عْمول هيْك.
Hazem, do it like this.

شِفِت شو عامْلين بِالجْنيْنِة؟
Did you see what they've done in the garden?

ما عْمِلْنا السّهْرة لأنّ صار في مشْكل بِالحارة.
We didn't have the party because a problem happened in the neighborhood.

63 *sound measure II* to wash غَسَّل

	perfect		imperfect		bi-imperfect	
ána	*ɣassálit*	غَسَّلت	*ɣássil*	غَسِّل	*bɣássil*	بْغَسِّل
níḫna	*ɣassálna*	غَسَّلْنا	*nɣássil*	نْغَسِّل	*minɣássil*	مِنْغَسِّل
ínta	*ɣassálit*	غَسَّلت	*tɣássil*	تْغَسِّل	*bitɣássil*	بِتْغَسِّل
ínti	*ɣassálti*	غَسَّلْتي	*tɣássli*	تْغَسّْلي	*bitɣássli*	بِتْغَسّْلي
íntu	*ɣassáltu*	غَسَّلْتوا	*tɣásslu*	تْغَسّْلوا	*bitɣásslu*	بِتْغَسّْلوا
húwwi	*ɣással*	غَسَّل	*yɣássil*	يْغَسِّل	*biɣássil*	بيغَسِّل
híyyi	*ɣássalit*	غَسَّلت	*tɣássil*	تْغَسِّل	*bitɣássil*	بِتْغَسِّل
hínni	*ɣássalu*	غَسَّلوا	*yɣásslu*	يْغَسّْلوا	*biɣásslu*	بيغَسّْلوا

	imperative	
ínta	*ɣássil*	غَسِّل
ínti	*ɣássli*	غَسّْلي
íntu	*ɣásslu*	غَسّْلوا

	active participle	
masculine	*mɣássil*	مْغَسِّل
feminine	*mɣássli*	مْغَسّْلِة
plural	*mɣásslīn*	مْغَسّْلين

سلامِة غسّل كْلاويه مِن كم يوْم.

Salama underwent kidney dialysis [lit. washed his kidneys] a few days ago.

إخْتي عم تْغسِّل الأواعي، منّا فاضْيِة.

My sister is busy doing the laundry.

ماهِر بْيِشْتِغِل بمِحطّة بيغسِّل فِيا السِّيّارات.

Maher works at a car wash [lit. station where he washes cars].

ما بْغسِّل بإِيدي أبداً.

I never wash [dishes] by hand!

الشّغّيلِة مْغسّْلين إزاز المحلّ و بْيِلْمع لمع.

The employees have cleaned the shop window and now it's shining.

to change غَيَّر

	perfect		imperfect		bi-imperfect	
ána	*ɣayyárit*	غَيَّرِت	*ɣáyyir*	غَيِّر	*bɣáyyir*	بْغَيِّر
níħna	*ɣayyárna*	غَيَّرْنا	*nɣáyyir*	نْغَيِّر	*minɣáyyir*	مِنْغَيِّر
ínta	*ɣayyárit*	غَيَّرِت	*tɣáyyir*	تْغَيِّر	*bitɣáyyir*	بْتْغَيِّر
ínti	*ɣayyárti*	غَيَّرْتي	*tɣáyyri*	تْغَيّْري	*bitɣáyyri*	بِتْغَيّْري
íntu	*ɣayyártu*	غَيَّرْتوا	*tɣáyyru*	تْغَيّْروا	*bitɣáyyru*	بِتْغَيّْروا
húwwi	*ɣáyyar*	غَيَّر	*yɣáyyir*	يْغَيِّر	*biɣáyyir*	بيغَيِّر
híyyi	*ɣáyyarit*	غَيَّرِت	*tɣáyyir*	تْغَيِّر	*bitɣáyyir*	بْتْغَيِّر
hínni	*ɣáyyaru*	غَيَّروا	*yɣáyyru*	يْغَيّْروا	*biɣáyyru*	بيغَيّْروا

	imperative	
ínta	*ɣáyyir*	غيِّر
ínti	*ɣáyyri*	غيّْري
íntu	*ɣáyyru*	غيّْروا

	active participle	
masculine	*mɣáyyir*	مْغَيِّر
feminine	*mɣáyyra*	مْغَيّْرة
plural	*mɣayyrīn*	مْغَيّْرين

غيّروا مطارِحُن بِالصّفّ.

They changed their places in the class.

بْضلّ غيرِّ محطّةْ التِّلِفِزْيوْن.

I keep changing the TV channel.

بِتْغيّْروا أواعيْكُن باكْسْتيْج.

Change your costumes backstage.

لينا مْغيّْرة كْتير، ما عم تِتْصرّف مِتْل العادِة.

Lina has changed a lot; she isn't acting as usual.

ما غيّروا مشْروعُن.

They didn't change their plans.

65 *hollow measure I* **to wake up** فاق

	perfect		imperfect		bi-imperfect	
ána	*fíʔit*	فِقِت	*fīʔ*	فيق	*bfīʔ*	بْفيق
níḩna	*fíʔna*	فِقْنا	*nfīʔ*	نْفيق	*minfīʔ*	مِنْفيق
ínta	*fíʔit*	فِقِت	*tfīʔ*	تْفيق	*bitfīʔ*	بِتْفيق
ínti	*fíʔti*	فِقْتي	*tfīʔi*	تْفيقي	*bitfīʔi*	بِتْفيقي
íntu	*fíʔtu*	فِقْتوا	*tfīʔu*	تْفيقوا	*bitfīʔu*	بِتْفيقوا
húwwi	*fēʔ*	فاق	*yfīʔ*	يْفيق	*bifīʔ*	بيفيق
híyyi	*fēʔit*	فاقِت	*tfīʔ*	تْفيق	*bitfīʔ*	بِتْفيق
hínni	*fēʔu*	فاقوا	*yfīʔu*	يْفيقوا	*bifīʔu*	بيفيقوا

	imperative	
ínta	*fīʔ*	فيق
ínti	*fīʔi*	فيقي
íntu	*fīʔu*	فيقوا

	active participle	
masculine	*fēyiʔ*	فايِق
feminine	*fēyʔa*	فايْقة
plural	*fēyʔīn*	فايْقين

روحي شوفي بِنْتِك روْلا. فاقِت مِن النّوْم.

Go and check on your daughter, Rola. She's woken up.

كِلّ يوْم بسّ فيق بِتْحمّم.

Every day when I wake up, I take a shower

أيّ ساعة بِالعادِة بِتْفيق الصُّبُح؟

What time do you usually wake up in the morning?

ما فِقِت عالوَقِت وتْأخّرِت عالشِّغِل.

I didn't wake up on time and I was late for work.

لاقَيْتُن بعْدُن فايْقين عم يِلْعبوا بْلايْسْتيْشين.

I found them awake playing PlayStation.

 sound measure I **to open** فَتَح

	perfect		imperfect		bi-imperfect	
ána	*fatáħit*	فَتَحِت	*íftaħ*	إفْتَح	*bíftaħ*	بِفْتَح
níħna	*fatáħna*	فَتَحْنا	*níftaħ*	نِفْتَح	*mníftaħ*	مْنِفْتَح
ínta	*fatáħit*	فَتَحِت	*tíftaħ*	تِفْتَح	*btíftaħ*	بْتِفْتَح
ínti	*fatáħti*	فَتَحْتي	*tíftaħi*	تِفْتَحي	*btíftaħi*	بْتِفْتَحي
íntu	*fatáħtu*	فَتَحْتوا	*tíftaħu*	تِفْتَحوا	*btíftaħu*	بْتِفْتَحوا
húwwi	*fátaħ*	فَتَح	*yíftaħ*	يِفْتَح	*byíftaħ*	بْيِفْتَح
híyyi	*fátaħit*	فَتَحِت	*tíftaħ*	تِفْتَح	*btíftaħ*	بْتِفْتَح
hínni	*fátaħu*	فَتَحوا	*yíftaħu*	يِفْتَحوا	*byíftaħu*	بْيِفْتَحوا

	imperative	
ínta	*ftāħ*	فْتاح
ínti	*ftáħi*	فْتَحي
íntu	*ftáħu*	فْتَحوا

	active participle	
masculine	*fētiħ*	فاتِح
feminine	*fētħa*	فاتْحَة
plural	*fētħīn*	فاتْحين

فتحْنا مَوْضوع للنِّقاش عن العلاقات بِالمُجْتمع.

We opened the subject of social relationships for discussion.

ما فِيّو يِفْتح العِلْبِة بِالسِّكّينة.

He can't open the can with the knife.

دايْماً سمير بْيِفْتح عِلْبِة المارْتديلّا بِفتّاحِةْ العِلب.

Sameer always opens tins of mortadella with a can opener.

فْتاح الباب للضُّيوف.

Open the door for the guests.

فاتْحين حديث جانْبِة بِالمُحاضرة.

They are having a side conversation during the lecture.

67 *defective measure XI* to show فَرْجى

	perfect		imperfect		bi-imperfect	
ána	*farjēt*	فَرْجيْت	*fárji*	فَرْجي	*bfárji*	بْفَرْجي
níħna	*farjáyna*	فَرْجَيْنا	*nfárji*	نْفَرْجي	*minfárji*	مِنْفَرْجي
ínta	*farjēt*	فَرْجيْت	*tfárji*	تْفَرْجي	*bitfárji*	بِتْفَرْجي
ínti	*farjáyti*	فَرْجَيْتي	*tfárji*	تْفَرْجي	*bitfárji*	بِتْفَرْجي
íntu	*farjáytu*	فَرْجَيْتوا	*tfárju*	تْفَرْجوا	*bitfárju*	بِتْفَرْجوا
húwwi	*fárja*	فَرْجى	*yfárji*	يْفَرْجي	*bifárji*	بيفَرْجي
híyyi	*fárjit*	فَرْجِت	*tfárji*	تْفَرْجي	*bitfárji*	بِتْفَرْجي
hínni	*fárju*	فَرْجوا	*yfárju*	يْفَرْجوا	*bifárju*	بيفَرْجوا

	imperative	
ínta	*fárji*	فَرْجي
ínti	*fárji*	فَرْجي
íntu	*fárju*	فَرْجوا

	active participle	
masculine	*mfárji*	مْفَرْجي
feminine	*mfarjíyyi*	مْفَرْجِيّة
plural	*mfarjiyyīn*	مْفَرْجِيّين

حسن فرْجى عضلاتو عالإنْسْتغْرام.
Hassan showed off his muscles on Instagram.

كارول، ما تْفرْجي حدا فُسْتانِك. خلّيا مُفاجئة.
Carol, don't show anyone your [wedding] dress. Keep it a surprise.

أيْ واللهِ بْفرْجي لَجوْنيّ برّات المدْرسِة.
I swear I will show Johnny [who's boss] after school.

فرْجي الإكْسسْوارات يَلّي شغّل إيديْك بِالمعْرض.
Show your handmade accessories at the exhibition.

عْمول معْروف فيك تْفرْجيني هَيْدي التّنّورة.
Can you please show me that skirt?

to think فَكَّر

	perfect		imperfect		bi-imperfect	
ána	*fakkárit*	فَكَّرِت	*fákkir*	فَكِّر	*bfákkir*	بْفَكِّر
níḫna	*fakkárna*	فَكَّرْنا	*nfákkir*	نْفَكِّر	*minfákkir*	مِنْفَكِّر
ínta	*fakkárit*	فَكَّرِت	*tfákkir*	تْفَكِّر	*bitfákkir*	بِتْفَكِّر
ínti	*fakkárti*	فَكَّرْتي	*tfákkri*	تْفَكّْري	*bitfákkri*	بِتْفَكّْري
íntu	*fakkártu*	فَكَّرْتوا	*tfákkru*	تْفَكّْروا	*bitfákkru*	بِتْفَكّْروا
húwwi	*fákkar*	فَكَّر	*yfákkir*	يْفَكِّر	*bifákkir*	بيفَكِّر
híyyi	*fákkarit*	فَكَّرِت	*tfákkir*	تْفَكِّر	*bitfákkir*	بِتْفَكِّر
hínni	*fákkaru*	فَكَّروا	*yfákkru*	يْفَكّْروا	*bifákkru*	بيفَكّْروا

	imperative	
ínta	*fákkir*	فَكِّر
ínti	*fákkri*	فَكّْري
íntu	*fákkru*	فَكّْروا

	active participle	
masculine	*mfákkir*	مْفَكِّر
feminine	*mfákkra*	مْفَكّْرَة
plural	*mfakkrīn*	مْفَكّْرين

فكّرْتك جايِة اليوْم.
I thought you were coming today.

عم تْفكِّر فيك.
She's thinking of you.

ما بِتْفكِّر أَوْقات بِالسّبب وَرا كِلّ هَيْدا؟
Don't you wonder sometimes about the reason behind all this?

مْفكّْرين إنّو العُطْلِة بعْد أُسْبوع.
They thought that the holiday is in a week.

فكّْري بْجَواب هَيْدا السُّؤال.
Think of an answer to this question.

to understand

	perfect		imperfect		bi-imperfect	
ána	*fhímit*	فْهِمت	*ífham*	إفْهَم	*bífham*	بِفْهَم
níḫna	*fhímna*	فْهِمْنا	*nífham*	نِفْهَم	*mnífham*	مْنِفْهَم
ínta	*fhímit*	فْهِمت	*tífham*	تِفْهَم	*btífham*	بْتِفْهَم
ínti	*fhímti*	فْهِمْتي	*tífhami*	تِفْهَمي	*btífhami*	بْتِفْهَمي
íntu	*fhímtu*	فْهِمْتوا	*tífhamu*	تِفْهَموا	*btífhamu*	بْتِفْهَموا
húwwi	*fíhim*	فِهِم	*yífham*	يِفْهَم	*byífham*	بْيِفْهَم
híyyi	*fíhmit*	فِهْمِت	*tífham*	تِفْهَم	*btífham*	بْتِفْهَم
hínni	*fíhmu*	فِهْموا	*yífhamu*	يِفْهَموا	*byífhamu*	بْيِفْهَموا

	imperative	
ínta	*fhām*	فْهام
ínti	*fhámi*	فْهَمي
íntu	*fhámu*	فْهَموا

	active participle	
masculine	*fēhim*	فاهِم
feminine	*fēhmi*	فاهْمِة
plural	*fēhmīn*	فاهْمين

الطُّلاب فِهْموا درْس التّاريخ مْنيح.

The students understood the history lesson well.

ما بعْرِف إحْكي إنْكْليزي بسّ بِفْهم عليْك.

I can't speak English, but I can understand you.

ميرا بْتِفْهم بْهنْدسِةْ الكُمْبْيوتر.

Mira knows computer engineering.

فْهام مِن بيّك شو بدّو مِنّك.

Make sure you understand what your father wants from you.

دِقّي لصاحْبِك فْهمي مِنّو أيمْتى العُطْلِة.

Call your friend to find out when the vacation starts.

to say قال

	perfect		imperfect		bi-imperfect	
ána	*ʔílit*	قِلت	*ʔūl*	قول	*bʔūl*	بْقول
níħna	*ʔílna*	قِلنا	*nʔūl*	نْقول	*minʔūl*	مِنْقول
ínta	*ʔílit*	قِلت	*tʔūl*	تْقول	*bitʔūl*	بِتْقول
ínti	*ʔílti*	قِلْتي	*tʔūli*	تْقولي	*bitʔūli*	بِتْقولي
íntu	*ʔíltu*	قِلْتوا	*tʔūlu*	تْقولوا	*bitʔūlu*	بِتْقولوا
húwwi	*ʔāl*	قال	*yʔūl*	يْقول	*biʔūl*	بيقول
híyyi	*ʔālit*	قالِت	*tʔūl*	تْقول	*bitʔūl*	بِتْقول
hínni	*ʔālu*	قالوا	*yʔūlu*	يْقولوا	*biʔūlu*	بيقولوا

	imperative	
ínta	*ʔūl*	قول
ínti	*ʔūli*	قولي
íntu	*ʔūlu*	قولوا

	active participle	
masculine	*ʔāyil*	قايِل
feminine	*ʔāyli*	قايْلِة
plural	*ʔāylīn*	قايْلين

قِلْنا ما رح نْعيد نفْس الغلْطة مرّة تانْيِة.
We agreed that we wouldn't make the same mistake again.

كِلّ مرّة بيقول لهادي نفْس القِصّة.
Every time, he tells Hadi the same story.

ليْه بِتْقولي إنّو ما عاد بِدِّك تِحْكي معي؟
Why are you saying that you don't want to talk to me?

قول إذا عِنْدك أيّ سُؤال بْهَيْدا الأُجْتِماع.
Tell [me] if you have any question during this meeting.

نورا ما قالِت لأحْمد شو السّبب الحقيقي.
Nora didn't tell Ahmed the real reason.

sound measure I

to earn

قَبَض

	perfect		imperfect		bi-imperfect	
ána	ʔabáḍit	قَبَضِت	íʔbaḍ	إقْبَض	bíʔbaḍ	بِقْبَض
níḫna	ʔabáḍna	قَبَضْنا	níʔbaḍ	نِقْبَض	mníʔbaḍ	مْنِقْبَض
ínta	ʔabáḍit	قَبَضِت	tíʔbaḍ	تِقْبَض	btíʔbaḍ	بْتِقْبَض
ínti	ʔabáḍti	قَبَضْتي	tíʔbaḍi	تِقْبَضي	btíʔbaḍi	بْتِقْبَضي
íntu	ʔabáḍtu	قَبَضْتوا	tíʔbaḍ	تِقْبَضوا	btíʔbaḍ	بْتِقْبَضوا
húwwi	ʔábaḍ	قَبَض	yíʔbaḍ	يِقْبَض	byíʔbaḍ	بْيِقْبَض
híyyi	ʔábaḍit	قَبَضِت	tíʔbaḍ	تِقْبَض	btíʔbaḍ	بْتِقْبَض
hínni	ʔábaḍu	قَبَضوا	yíʔbaḍu	يِقْبَضوا	byíʔbaḍu	بْيِقْبَضوا

	imperative	
ínta	ʔbāḍ	قْباض
ínti	ʔbáḍi	قْبَضي
íntu	ʔbáḍu	قْبَضوا

	active participle	
masculine	ʔābiḍ	قابِض
feminine	ʔābḍa	قابْضَة
plural	ʔābḍīn	قابْضين

ما بْيِقْبَض أتْعابو نْهايِة الخِدْمِة .
He doesn't get paid at the end of his service.

رح تِقْبَض بُكْرا معاشا بِالشِّغِل.
She will get paid tomorrow.

قبض معاش التّقاعُد مِن صنْدوق الضّمان الاِجْتِماعي.
He received his retirement pension from the Social Security Fund.

منال مِزْحِت مع مازِن وهُوِّ قبض المَوْضوع جد.
Manal joked with Mazen and he took it personally.

كان بدّو التّرْقية كِرْمال يِقْبض أكْتر بِشِغْلو.
He wanted the promotion so he could earn more at his job.

خلّيني إقْبض معاشي.
Let me earn my salary.

72 *sound measure I* **to kill** قَتَل

	perfect		imperfect		bi-imperfect	
ána	*ʔatálit*	قَتَلِت	*íʔtul*	إِقْتُل	*bíʔtul*	بِقْتُل
níḫna	*ʔatálna*	قَتَلْنا	*níʔtul*	نِقْتُل	*mníʔtul*	مْنِقْتُل
ínta	*ʔatálit*	قَتَلِت	*tíʔtul*	تِقْتُل	*btíʔtul*	بْتِقْتُل
ínti	*ʔatálti*	قَتَلْتي	*tíʔtli*	تِقْتْلي	*btíʔtli*	بْتِقْتْلي
íntu	*ʔátalu*	قَتَلْتوا	*tíʔtlu*	تِقْتْلوا	*btíʔtlu*	بْتِقْتْلوا
húwwi	*ʔátal*	قَتَل	*yíʔtul*	يِقْتُل	*byíʔtul*	بْيِقْتُل
híyyi	*ʔátalit*	قَتَلِت	*tíʔtul*	تِقْتُل	*btíʔtul*	بْتِقْتُل
hínni	*ʔátalu*	قَتَلوا	*yíʔtlu*	يِقْتْلوا	*byíʔtlu*	بْيِقْتْلوا

	imperative	
ínta	*ʔtūl*	قْتول
ínti	*ʔtíli*	قْتِلي
íntu	*ʔtílu*	قْتِلوا

	active participle	
masculine	*ʔētil*	قاتِل
feminine	*ʔētli*	قاتْلِة
plural	*ʔētlīn*	قاتْلين

⚠ Besides meaning 'kill' literally (first and third examples) or figuratively (second example), this verb also means 'fight (against)' (fourth and fifth examples).

أبو جاد قتل عمّو كِرْمال الورْثِة.

Abo Jad killed his uncle over inheritance issues.

بْتِقْتِلْني بْعْيونا بسّ شوفا.

She kills me with her eyes when I see her.

ليْش بْتِقْتْلوا العْصافير؟

Why do you kill birds?

قْتِلي كِلّ مين بْيِتْحرّش فيكي.

Fight whoever harasses you.

قدْ ما الشِّقّة لقْطة، في كْتير قاتْلين حالُم عليّا.

The apartment is such a hot deal that many are dying [lit. killing themselves] to get it.

73 *sound measure I* to be able to قِدِر

	perfect		imperfect		bi-imperfect	
ána	*ʔdírit*	قْدِرت	*íʔdar*	إقْدَر	*bíʔdar*	بِقْدَر
níḫna	*ʔdírna*	قْدِرْنا	*níʔdar*	نِقْدَر	*mníʔdar*	مْنِقْدَر
ínta	*ʔdírit*	قْدِرت	*tíʔdar*	تِقْدَر	*btíʔdar*	بْتِقْدَر
ínti	*ʔdírti*	قْدِرْتي	*tíʔdari*	تِقْدَري	*btíʔdari*	بْتِقْدَري
íntu	*ʔdírtu*	قْدِرْتوا	*tíʔdaru*	تِقْدَروا	*btíʔdaru*	بْتِقْدَروا
húwwi	*ʔídir*	قِدِر	*yíʔdar*	يِقْدَر	*byíʔdar*	بْيِقْدَر
híyyi	*ʔídrit*	قِدْرت	*tíʔdar*	تِقْدَر	*btíʔdar*	بْتِقْدَر
hínni	*ʔídru*	قِدْروا	*yíʔdaru*	يِقْدَروا	*byíʔdaru*	بْيِقْدَروا

	imperative	
ínta	*ʔdār*	قْدار
ínti	*ʔdári*	قْدَري
íntu	*ʔdáru*	قْدَروا

	active participle	
masculine	*ʔēdir*	قادِر
feminine	*ʔēdra*	قادْرَة
plural	*ʔēdrīn*	قادْرين

⚠ ➲ Compare with **T-103**.

بِقْدر إتْحمّل الشّغِل لَوَحْدي مِن دون مُساعدِة.
I can handle the work alone without any help.

قْدِرْتوا تْبيعوا الإكْسِسْوارات بْمعْرض أبو رُخّوصة؟
Were you able to sell the accessories at the Abo Rakhosa exhibition?

ما بْتِقْدر يا عامر تِجي لعِنّا عالضّيْعة بِالسّعديّات كِرْمال جِدّك ما يزْعل؟
Amer, can't you come to our house in the village Saadeyat
so that your grandfather doesn't get upset?

لمْيا بْتِقْدر تِكْتُب عالكُمْبْيوتر.
Lamia can type on the computer.

عبّاس بْيِقْدر يحْمُل أَوْزان تْقيلِة بِالنّادي.
Abbas can lift heavy weights at the gym.

شِفْلي إذا قادِر تعْمِلّي فرْضي.
See if you can do my homework.

يِمْكِن ما تِقْدَر تِجي عالسّهْرة.
She probably can't come to the party.

	perfect		imperfect		bi-imperfect	
ána	*ʔarēt*	قَريْت	*íʔra*	إقْرا	*bíʔra*	بِقْرا
níħna	*ʔaráyna*	قَرَيْنا	*níʔra*	نِقْرا	*mníʔra*	مْنِقْرا
ínta	*ʔarēt*	قَريْت	*tíʔra*	تِقْرا	*btíʔra*	بْتِقْرا
ínti	*ʔaráyti*	قَرَيْتي	*tíʔri*	تِقْري	*btíʔri*	بْتِقْري
íntu	*ʔaráytu*	قَرَيْتوا	*tíʔru*	تِقْروا	*btíʔru*	بْتِقْروا
húwwi	*ʔára*	قَرا	*yíʔra*	يِقْرا	*byíʔra*	بْيِقْرا
híyyi	*ʔárit*	قَرِت	*tíʔra*	تِقْرا	*btíʔra*	بْتِقْرا
hínni	*ʔáru*	قَروا	*yíʔru*	يِقْروا	*byíʔru*	بْيِقْروا

	imperative	
ínta	*ʔrā*	قْرا
ínti	*ʔrī*	قْري
íntu	*ʔrū*	قْروا

	active participle	
masculine	*ʔēri*	قاري
feminine	*ʔēryi*	قارْيِة
plural	*ʔēryīn*	قارْيين

⚠ The final *a* may be spelled ى or ا, depending on the verb (and an individual's spelling preferences).

قرا مسْرحِيّات لزِياد الرّحْباني.

He read plays by Ziad Rahbani.

شو عم تِقْري؟

What are you reading?

كِلّ يوْم بِقْرا جرايِد عالصُّبْح.

Every morning, I read newspapers.

ما بْتِقْروا قُصص بِالبيْت؟

Don't you read stories at home?

قارْيِة كِلّ رِوايات أمين معْلوف وجِبْران خليل جِبْران.

She has read all the novels by Amin Maalouf and Khalil Gibran.

sound measure I

to sit

قَعَد

	perfect		imperfect		bi-imperfect	
ána	ʔa3ádit	قَعَدِت	íʔ3ud	إقْعُد	bíʔ3ud	بِقْعُد
níḫna	ʔa3ádna	قَعَدْنا	níʔ3ud	نِقْعُد	mníʔ3ud	مْنِقْعُد
ínta	ʔa3ádit	قَعَدِت	tíʔ3ud	تِقْعُد	btíʔ3ud	بْتِقْعُد
ínti	ʔa3ádti	قَعَدْتي	tíʔ3di	تِقْعْدي	btíʔ3di	بْتِقْعْدي
íntu	ʔa3ádtu	قَعَدْتوا	tíʔ3du	تِقْعْدوا	btíʔ3du	بْتِقْعْدوا
húwwi	ʔá3ad	قَعَد	yíʔ3ud	يِقْعُد	byíʔ3ud	بْيِقْعُد
híyyi	ʔá3adit	قَعَدِت	tíʔ3ud	تِقْعُد	btíʔ3ud	بْتِقْعُد
hínni	ʔá3adu	قَعَدوا	yíʔ3du	يِقْعْدوا	byíʔ3du	بْيِقْعْدوا

	imperative	
ínta	ʔ3ād	قْعاد
ínti	ʔ3ídi	قْعِدي
íntu	ʔ3ídu	قْعِدوا

	active participle	
masculine	ʔē3id	قاعِد
feminine	ʔē3di	قاعْدِة
plural	ʔē3dīn	قاعْدين

مِن أُسْبوع قعدْنا عِنْد قهْوِة أبو نِزار ولْعِبْنا طاوْلِة زهر.
A week ago, we went to Abu Nizar café and played backgammon.

بْيِقْعْدوا عَ الكراسي بِالمسْرح.
They are sitting in chairs in the theater.

حاجِة تِقْعُد تعْمِلّي فِيا فهْمان كِلّ شي.
Stop acting like you know everything.

جميل، ما تِقْعُد بْآخِر الصّفّ، قرِّب لقِدّام.
Jamil, don't sit in the back row. Come up to the front!

رح نِقْعُد بْبيْروت لشهِر.
We're going to stay in Beirut for a month.

المُوَظّفين قاعْدين يْتِمتْموا بِالمكْتب.
The employees are gossiping in the office.

بِقْعُد بِسْهر للصُّبْح بِسْمع فيْروز.
I stay awake until morning listening to Fayrouz.

بِقْعُد أيّام الأحد بلا شِغِل.
I don't work on Sundays.

76^A *defective measure I* **to be** كان

	perfect		imperfect		bi-imperfect	
ána	*kínit*	كِنِت	*kūn*	كون	*bkūn*	بْكون
níḫna	*kínna*	كِنّا	*nkūn*	نْكون	*minkūn*	مِنْكون
ínta	*kínit*	كِنِت	*tkūn*	تْكون	*bitkūn*	بِتْكون
ínti	*kínti*	كِنْتي	*tkūni*	تْكوني	*bitkūni*	بِتْكوني
íntu	*kíntu*	كِنْتوا	*tkūnu*	تْكونوا	*bitkūnu*	بِتْكونوا
húwwi	*kēn*	كان	*ykūn*	يْكون	*bikūn*	بيكون
híyyi	*kēnit*	كانِت	*tkūn*	تْكون	*bitkūn*	بِتْكون
hínni	*kēnu*	كانوا	*ykūnu*	يْكونوا	*bikūnu*	بيكونوا

	imperative	
ínta	*kūn*	كون
ínti	*kūni*	كوني
íntu	*kūnu*	كونوا

	active participle	
masculine	*kēyin*	كاين
feminine	*kēyni*	كايْنِة
plural	*kēynīn*	كايْنين

⚠

① The bi-imperfect of this verb is used for habits or the future, as in examples 3 and 5 below.

② To express *to be* (*am, is, are*) in the present tense, see the next page.

③ A perfect or imperfect form of this verb follows another verb to create a compound tense. ➲ **Compound Tenses** *p. 114*

كان بيحِبّ يِقْعُد بْهاي الكافيْه.

He used to like sitting in this café.

كِلّ مرّة بِتْكون لَوَحْدا بِالجُنيْنِة.

She is always alone in the garden.

بسّ تْكونوا سَوا خْدولْكُن صورة.

When you're together, take a photo.

ما بْكون بِالبيْت بعْد الضُّهُر.

I won't be at home in the afternoon.

كون شي مرّة حدا مْهِمّ بْحَياتك.

For once, be in charge of your own life.

ما كِنّا مشْغولين مْبارِح.

We weren't very busy yesterday.

كوني ذكية وقَوية.

Be smart and strong.

am/is/are (not) كان

positive		negative	
ána	أَنا	*mánni*	مَنّي
níħna	نِحْنا	*mánna*	مَنّا
ínta	إِنْتَ	*mánnak*	مَنّك
ínti	إِنْتي	*mánnik*	مَنِّك
íntu	إِنْتو	*mánnkun*	منْكُن
húwwi	هُوِّ	*mánnu*	مَنّو
híyyi	هِيِّ	*mánna*	مَنّا
hínni	هِنِّ	*mánnun*	مَنُّن
		miš	مِش

⚠

① There is no equivalent of *am, is, are.* It is simply absent from the sentence. For example, *'The book is on the table. It is heavy.'* would literally be *'The book on the table. It heavy.'*
② The subject can be an independent pronoun, shown in the table on the left and in the examples below.
③ The subject noun or pronoun is followed by مِش *miš* in the negative (*am not, isn't, aren't*). An independent pronoun and مِش *miš* can be replaced by a special negative form, shown on the right side of the table.

أنا مِن لِبْنان.
I am from Lebanon.

إِنْتَ وَيْن؟
Where are you?

هِيِّ فنّانِة مشْهورة بْلِبْنان.
She is a famous Lebanese singer.

نِحْنا هون.
We are here.

هِنِّ رِفْقاتي.
They are my good friends.

لَيْش منُّن جايين لعِنّا؟
Why aren't they coming to visit us?

هِيِّ منّا مْعلّْمِة.
She is not a teacher.

منّي مشْغول.
I am not busy.

منْكُن قادْرين تِحِمْلوا الصّوفا؟
Aren't you able to carry the sofa?

هُوِّ منّو مِن بيْروت.
He is not from Beirut.

⚠ The verb كان *kēn* is also used in prepositional constructions. ➲ T-98-103

77 *sound measure I* **to write** 

	perfect		imperfect		bi-imperfect	
ána	*katábit*	كَتَبِت	*íktub*	إكْتُب	*bíktub*	بِكْتُب
níḫna	*katábna*	كَتَبْنا	*níktub*	نِكْتُب	*mníktub*	مْنِكْتُب
ínta	*katábit*	كَتَبِت	*tíktub*	تِكْتُب	*btíktub*	بْتِكْتُب
ínti	*katábti*	كَتَبْتي	*tíktbi*	تِكْتْبي	*btíktbi*	بْتِكْتْبي
íntu	*katábtu*	كتبتوا	*tíktbu*	تِكْتْبوا	*btíktbu*	بْتِكْتْبوا
húwwi	*kátab*	كَتَب	*yíktub*	يِكْتُب	*byíktub*	بْيِكْتُب
híyyi	*kátabit*	كَتَبِت	*tíktub*	تِكْتُب	*btíktub*	بْتِكْتُب
hínni	*kátabu*	كَتَبوا	*yíktbu*	يِكْتْبوا	*byíktbu*	بْيِكْتْبوا

	imperative	
ínta	*ktūb*	كْتوب
ínti	*ktíbi*	كْتِبي
íntu	*ktíbu*	كْتِبوا

	active participle	
masculine	*kētib*	كاتِب
feminine	*kētbi*	كاتْبِة
plural	*kētbīn*	كاتْبين

ما بِقْدر إكْتُب عربي، بسّ بعْرِف إحْكي مْنيح.
I can't write Arabic, but I speak [it] well.

شو عم تِكْتُب؟
What are you writing?

نور بْتِكْتُب مُذكراتا كِلّ يوْم.
Nour writes in her diary every day.

كْتوب اِسْمك على هَيْدا السّطِر.
Write your name on this line.

خليل جِبْران ما كتب كْتاب" النّبي "بِالعربي، هُوِّ كتبو بِالإنْكْليزي.
Kahlil Gibran didn't write his book "The Prophet" in Arabic. He wrote it in English.

اليوْم لازِم تِكْتْبوا دْروسْكُن بِالبيْت.
Today, you should do your schoolwork at home.

كتبوا على حيْطان المدْرسِة.
They wrote on the walls of the school.

sound measure II

to lie

كَذَّب

	perfect		imperfect		bi-imperfect	
ána	*kazzábit*	كَذَّبِت	*kázzib*	كَذِّب	*bkázzib*	بْكَذِّب
níḫna	*kazzábna*	كَذَّبْنا	*nkázzib*	نْكَذِّب	*minkázzib*	مِنْكَذِّب
ínta	*kazzábit*	كَذَّبِت	*tkázzib*	تْكَذِّب	*bitkázzib*	بِتْكَذِّب
ínti	*kazzábti*	كَذَّبْتي	*tkázzbi*	تْكَذّْبي	*bitkázzbi*	بِتْكَذّْبي
íntu	*kazzábtu*	كَذَّبْتوا	*tkázzbu*	تْكَذّْبوا	*bitkázzbu*	بِتْكَذّْبوا
húwwi	*kázzab*	كَذَّب	*ykázzib*	يْكَذِّب	*bikázzib*	بيْكَذِّب
híyyi	*kázzabit*	كَذَّبِت	*tkázzib*	تْكَذِّب	*bitkázzib*	بِتْكَذِّب
hínni	*kázzabu*	كَذَّبوا	*ykázzbu*	يْكَذّْبوا	*bikázzbu*	بيْكَذّْبوا

	imperative	
ínta	*kázzib*	كَذِّب
ínti	*kázzbi*	كَذّْبي
íntu	*kázzbu*	كَذّْبوا

	active participle	
masculine	*mkázzib*	مْكَذِّب
feminine	*mkázzbi*	مْكَذّْبِة
plural	*mkazzbīn*	مْكَذّْبين

كذّبِت عَ البابا لَيْخلّيني إطْلع معْكُن.

I lied to my father, so he'd let me go out with you.

حاجِة تْكَذِّب علينْا.

Stop lying to us!

ما تْصدِّق السِّياسية كِلُّن، بيكذّْبوا علينْا.

Never trust all the politicians. They lie to us.

ما تْكذِّب علَيا وخلّيك صريح معا.

Never lie to her. Just be honest with her.

كذّْبي لمّا تْروحي عالمُقابلِة.

Lie when you go to the job interview.

79 *hollow measure III* **to find** لاقى

	perfect		imperfect		bi-imperfect	
ána	*lēʔēt*	لاقيْت	*lēʔi*	لاقي	*blēʔi*	بْلاقي
níḫna	*lēʔáyna*	لاقَيْنا	*nlēʔi*	نْلاقي	*minlēʔi*	مِنْلاقي
ínta	*lēʔēt*	لاقيْت	*tlēʔi*	تْلاقي	*bitlēʔi*	بِتْلاقي
ínti	*lēʔáyti*	لاقَيْتي	*tlēʔi*	تْلاقي	*bitlēʔi*	بِتْلاقي
íntu	*lēʔáytu*	لاقَيْتوا	*tlēʔu*	تْلاقوا	*bitlēʔu*	بِتْلاقوا
húwwi	*lēʔa*	لاقى	*ylēʔi*	يْلاقي	*bilēʔi*	بيلاقي
híyyi	*lēʔit*	لاقِت	*tlēʔi*	تْلاقي	*bitlēʔi*	بِتْلاقي
hínni	*lēʔu*	لاقوا	*ylēʔu*	يْلاقوا	*bilēʔu*	بيلاقوا

	imperative	
ínta	*lēʔi*	لاقي
ínti	*lēʔi*	لاقي
íntu	*lēʔu*	لاقوا

	active participle	
masculine	*mlēʔi*	مْلاقي
feminine	*mlēʔyi*	مْلاقْية
plural	*mlēʔyīn*	مْلاقْيين

⚠ The perfect forms are also commonly spelled without the alif (ا): لقى

كْريسْتين، لاقَيْتي غِنّيةْ زِياد بُرْجي؟
Christine, did you find the song by Ziad Bourji?

جوْ! عْمول معْروف لاقي مْفاتيح لبيْت.
Joe! Please, find the house keys.

لاقوا صبي مْضيِّع أهْلو بِالدّامور.
They found a lost boy in Damour.

سوْري، بْلاقي عِنْدك مِن هَيْدا الشّامْبو؟
Excuse me, can I find this kind of shampoo here?

ما بِتْلاقي مِن هَيْدا السّينْسيل إلّا عِنْد بَيْروت موْل.
You can't find this necklace anywhere except in Beirut Mall.

sound measure I

to wear

لِبِس

	perfect		imperfect		bi-imperfect	
ána	*lbísit*	لْبِسِت	*ílbus*	إِلْبُس	*bílbus*	بِلْبُس
níḫna	*lbísna*	لْبِسْنا	*nílbus*	نِلْبُس	*mnílbus*	مْنِلْبُس
ínta	*lbísit*	لْبِسِت	*tílbus*	تِلْبُس	*btílbus*	بْتِلْبُس
ínti	*lbísti*	لْبِسْتي	*tílbsi*	تِلْبْسي	*btílbsi*	بْتِلْبْسي
íntu	*lbístu*	لْبِسْتوا	*tílbsu*	تِلْبْسوا	*btílbsu*	بْتِلْبْسوا
húwwi	*líbis*	لِبِس	*yílbus*	يِلْبُس	*byílbus*	بْيِلْبُس
híyyi	*líbsit*	لِبْسِت	*tílbus*	تِلْبُس	*btílbus*	بْتِلْبُس
hínni	*líbsu*	لِبْسوا	*yílbsu*	يِلْبْسوا	*byílbsu*	بْيِلْبْسوا

	imperative	
ínta	*lbūs*	لْبوس
ínti	*lbísi*	لْبِسي
íntu	*lbísu*	لْبِسوا

	active participle	
masculine	*lēbis*	لابِس
feminine	*lēbsi*	لابْسِة
plural	*lēbsīn*	لابْسين

حكيْت مع جلال، رح يِلْبُس كنْزتو ويِلْحقْنا.
I talked to Jalal. He's going to put on a sweater and come with us.

جِنان لِبْسِت تنّورة بِتْجنِّن.
Jinan wore a beautiful skirt.

بْحِبّ الْبُس رسْمي لمّا روح على الاِجْتِماع.
I like to dress formally when I go to a meeting.

لِبِس بْقلْب هَيْدي الغِرْفِة لنْشوف كيف القِياس طالع عليْك.
Try it on in the fitting room to see how it looks on you.

الجُمْهور بِالملْعب لابْسين ذات الألْوان.
The spectators in the stadium are wearing the same colors.

كان لابِس طقِم وكْرافات لمّا شِفْتو مْبارِح.
He was wearing a suit and tie when I saw him yesterday.

شو لابْسِة؟
What are you wearing?

81 *sound measure I* **to play** لِعِب

	perfect		imperfect		bi-imperfect	
ána	*l3íbit*	لْعِبِت	*íl3ab*	إِلْعَب	*bíl3ab*	بِلْعَب
níħna	*l3íbna*	لْعِبْنا	*níl3ab*	نِلْعَب	*mníl3ab*	مْنِلْعَب
ínta	*l3íbit*	لْعِبِت	*tíl3ab*	تِلْعَب	*btíl3ab*	بْتِلْعَب
ínti	*l3íbti*	لْعِبْتي	*tíl3abi*	تِلْعَبي	*btíl3abi*	بْتِلْعَبي
íntu	*l3íbtu*	لْعِبْتوا	*tíl3abu*	تِلْعَبوا	*btíl3abu*	بْتِلْعَبوا
húwwi	*lí3ib*	لِعِب	*yíl3ab*	يِلْعَب	*byíl3ab*	بْيِلْعَب
híyyi	*lí3bit*	لِعْبِت	*tíl3ab*	تِلْعَب	*btíl3ab*	بْتِلْعَب
hínni	*lí3bu*	لِعْبوا	*yíl3abu*	يِلْعَبوا	*byíl3abu*	بْيِلْعَبوا

	imperative	
ínta	*l3āb*	لْعاب
ínti	*l3ábi*	لْعَبي
íntu	*l3ábu*	لْعَبوا

	active participle	
masculine	*lē3ib*	لاعِب
feminine	*lē3bi*	لاعْبِة
plural	*lē3bīn*	لاعْبين

هالفريق لِعْبوا كْتير مْنيح مْبارِح بِالملْعب.

This team played very well yesterday at the stadium.

عم بِلْعب بْلايْسْتيْشين.

I'm playing Playstation

بْتِلْعبي معي بيْت بْيوت؟

Do you want to play house with me?

روح لْعاب بْعيد عنّي.

Go play somewhere else [away from me].

ما بِترْك الوْلاد لَوَحْدُن يِلْعبوا بِالطّريق.

I don't let the children play alone in the street.

	perfect		imperfect		bi-imperfect	
ána	*masákit*	مَسَكِت	*ímsuk*	إمْسُك	*bímsuk*	بِمْسُك
níħna	*masákna*	مَسَكْنا	*nímsuk*	نِمْسُك	*mnímsuk*	مْنِمْسُك
ínta	*masákit*	مَسَكِت	*tímsuk*	تِمْسُك	*btímsuk*	بْتِمْسُك
ínti	*masákti*	مَسَكْتي	*tímski*	تِمْسْكي	*btímski*	بْتِمْسْكي
íntu	*masáktu*	مَسَكْتوا	*tímsku*	تِمْسْكوا	*btímsku*	بْتِمْسْكوا
húwwi	*másak*	مَسَك	*yímsuk*	يِمْسُك	*byímsuk*	بْيِمْسُك
híyyi	*másakit*	مَسَكِت	*tímsuk*	تِمْسُك	*btímsuk*	بْتِمْسُك
hínni	*másaku*	مَسَكوا	*yímsku*	يِمْسْكوا	*byímsku*	بْيِمْسْكوا

	imperative	
ínta	*msūk*	مْسوك
ínti	*msíki*	مْسِكي
íntu	*msíku*	مْسِكوا

	active participle	
masculine	*mēsik*	ماسِك
feminine	*mēski*	ماسْكِة
plural	*mēskīn*	ماسْكين

⚠ This particular verb can also be conjugated according to the **1s6** pattern, with the perfect forms taking kasra (ِ *i*): مِسِك *mísik*

مسكوا إيديْن بعضْن وغنّوا سَوا.

They held each other's hands and sang together.

مْسوك كِبّايْتي تَإرْبُط صُبّاطي.

Hold my cup while I tie my shoe

الطِّفْل روني ما بْيِمْسُك حالو بِاللّيْل وبْيَعْمِلا تحْتو.

The child Roni cannot control himself at night and wets his bed.

بْحِبّ إمْسُك مسْبْحة بِإيدي.

I like holding a rosary in my hand.

ليْش ماسِك السِّلُّم بالعرِض!

Why are you taking life so seriously [lit. holding the ladder to the ground]?

83 *defective measure I* **to walk** مِشي

	perfect		imperfect		bi-imperfect	
ána	*mšīt*	مْشيت	*ímši*	إِمْشي	*bímši*	بِـمْشي
níḫna	*mšīna*	مْشينا	*nímši*	نِـمْشي	*mnímši*	مْنِمْشي
ínta	*mšīt*	مْشيت	*tímši*	تِـمْشي	*btímši*	بْتِمْشي
ínti	*mšīti*	مْشيتي	*tímši*	تِـمْشي	*btímši*	بْتِمْشي
íntu	*mšītu*	مْشيتوا	*tímšu*	تِـمْشوا	*btímšu*	بْتِمْشوا
húwwi	*míši*	مِشي	*yímši*	يِـمشي	*byímši*	بْيِمْشي
híyyi	*míšyit*	مِشْيِت	*tímši*	تِـمْشي	*btímši*	بْتِمْشي
hínni	*míšyu*	مِشْيوا	*yímšu*	يِـمشوا	*byímšu*	بْيِمْشوا

	imperative	
ínta	*mšī*	مْشي
ínti	*mšī*	مْشي
íntu	*mšū*	مْشوا

	active participle	
masculine	*mēši*	ماشي
feminine	*mēšyi*	ماشْيِة
plural	*mēšyīn*	ماشْيين

مْشيت عالرَّوْشِة مع أصْحابي.

I walked along the Raouché with my friends.

شو رأْيَك بْشِغِل مْراد؟ بْيِمْشي الحال تْخلّيه يْكمِّل بِالمُؤَسّسِة؟

What do you think about Mourad's work? Is it okay if you keep him in the company?

حاسِّة بمْعِدْتي ماشْيِة.

I have an upset stomach.

بِدّا تمْشي بْحِرْش بيرْوت.

She wants to go for a walk in Horsh Beirut.

مْشي بْعيد عنّي.

Get away from me!

to sleep نام

	perfect		imperfect		bi-imperfect	
ána	*nímit*	نمِت	*nēm*	نام	*bnēm*	بْنام
níḥna	*nímna*	نمِْنا	*nnēm*	نْنام	*minnēm*	مِنْنام
ínta	*nímit*	نمِت	*tnēm*	تْنام	*bitnēm*	بِتْنام
ínti	*nímti*	نمِْتي	*tnēmi*	تْنامي	*bitnēmi*	بِتْنامي
íntu	*nímtu*	نمِْتوا	*tnēmu*	تْناموا	*bitnēmu*	بِتْناموا
húwwi	*nēm*	نام	*ynēm*	يْنام	*binēm*	بينام
híyyi	*nēmit*	نامِت	*tnēm*	تْنام	*bitnēm*	بِتْنام
hínni	*nēmu*	ناموا	*ynēmu*	يْناموا	*binēmu*	بيناموا

	imperative	
ínta	*nēm*	نام
ínti	*nēmi*	نامي
íntu	*nēmu*	ناموا

	active participle	
masculine	*nēyim*	نايِم
feminine	*nēymi*	نايْمة
plural	*nēymīn*	نايْمين

بِالعادِة بْنام حَوالي السّبِع ساعات بِاللّيْلِة.
I usually sleep around seven hours a night.

ما قْدِرْنا نْنام اللّيْلِة لَأنّ الكلْب عم يْعوّي.
We couldn't sleep last night because of the barking dog.

روق، البيْبي نايِم.
Be quiet! The baby is sleeping.

كانِت تْنام بْتخِت بيّا وإمّا مِن لمّا كانِت صْغيرِة.
She used to sleep in her parents' bed when she was little.

جوْ ما نام مْبارِح بْغِرْفْتو.
Jo didn't sleep in his room last night.

85 *sound measure VII* **to enjoy** نْبَسَط

	perfect		imperfect		bi-imperfect	
ána	*nbasáṭit*	نْبَسَطِت	*unbúsiṭ*	أُنْبُسِط	*bunbúsiṭ*	بُنْبُسِط
níħna	*nbasáṭna*	نْبَسَطْنا	*nunbúsiṭ*	نُنْبُسِط	*mnunbúsiṭ*	مْنُنْبُسِط
ínta	*nbasáṭit*	نْبَسَطِت	*tunbúsiṭ*	تُنْبُسِط	*btunbúsiṭ*	بْتُنْبُسِط
ínti	*nbasáṭti*	نْبَسَطْتي	*tunbúsṭi*	تُنْبُسْطي	*btunbúsṭi*	بْتُنْبُسْطي
íntu	*nbasáṭtu*	نْبَسَطْتوا	*tunbúsṭu*	تُنْبُسْطوا	*btunbúsṭu*	بْتُنْبُسْطوا
húwwi	*nbásaṭ*	نْبَسَط	*yunbúsiṭ*	يُنْبُسِط	*byunbúsiṭ*	بْيُنْبُسِط
híyyi	*nbásṭit*	نْبَسْطِت	*tunbúsiṭ*	تُنْبُسِط	*btunbúsiṭ*	بْتُنْبُسِط
hínni	*nbásṭu*	نْبَسْطوا	*yunbúsṭu*	يُنْبُسْطوا	*byunbúsṭu*	بْيُنْبُسْطوا

	imperative	
ínta	*nbúsiṭ*	نْبُسِط
ínti	*nbúsṭi*	نْبُسْطي
íntu	*nbúsṭu*	نْبُسْطوا

	active participle	
masculine	*mabsūṭ*	مَبْسوط
feminine	*mabsūṭa*	مَبْسوطَة
plural	*mabsūṭīn*	مَبْسوطين

نْبسطِت بْشَوْفْتك.

I'm happy to see you.

شو لمى، بْتُنْبُسْطي لمّا تِسْمعي صَوْتو؟

Hey, Lama. Do you enjoy hearing his voice?

بْيُنْبُسْطوا الوْلاد بسّ ناخُدْن على حِرِش بيْروت.

The children enjoy it when we take them to Horsh Beirut.

ما مِنْبُسِط بْسهْرِة مْبارِح.

He didn't enjoy the party last night.

نْبُسِط بْعيد ميلادك مع رِفْقاتك بِالمطْعم.

Enjoy your birthday with your friends in the restaurant.

to forget نِسي

	perfect		imperfect		bi-imperfect	
ána	*nsīt*	نْسيت	*ínsa*	إِنْسا	*bínsa*	بِنْسا
niḫna	*nsīna*	نْسينا	*nínsa*	نِنْسا	*mnínsa*	مْنِنْسا
ínta	*nsīt*	نْسيت	*tínsa*	تِنْسا	*btínsa*	بْتِنْسا
ínti	*nsīti*	نْسيتي	*tínsi*	تِنْسي	*btínsi*	بْتِنْسي
íntu	*nsītu*	نْسيتوا	*tínsu*	تِنْسوا	*btínsu*	بْتِنْسوا
húwwi	*nísi*	نِسي	*yínsa*	يِنْسا	*byínsa*	بْيِنْسا
híyyi	*nísyit*	نِسْيِت	*tínsa*	تِنْسا	*btínsa*	بْتِنْسا
hínni	*nísyu*	نِسْيوا	*yínsu*	يِنْسوا	*byínsu*	بْيِنْسوا

	imperative	
ínta	*nsā*	نْسا
ínti	*nsī*	نْسي
íntu	*nsū*	نْسوا

	active participle	
masculine	*nēsi*	ناسي
feminine	*nēsyi*	ناسْيِة
plural	*nēsyīn*	ناسْيين

نْسينا المصاري بِالبيْت.

We forgot the money at the house.

ما تِنْسي تْجيبي مْفاتيح السِّيّارة معِك.

Don't forget to bring your car keys with you.

دايماً بِنْسا إكْتُب اِسْمي على وَرقةِ الاِمْتِحان.

I always forget to write my name on the exam paper.

نْسو القُصّة لأنّو مِش حقيقي.

Forget the story because it's not true.

كِلّ مرّة بْيِنْسوا يْجيبولي هْدية مْن السّفر.

They forget to bring me a gift each time they travel.

87 *geminate measure VII* **to join** نْضَمّ

	perfect		imperfect		bi-imperfect	
ána	*nḍammēt*	نْضَمّيْت	*indámm*	إنْضَمّ	*bindámm*	بِنْضَمّ
níħna	*nḍammáyna*	نْضَمّيْنا	*nindámm*	نِنْضَمّ	*mnindámm*	مْنِنْضَمّ
ínta	*nḍammēt*	نْضَمّيْت	*tindámm*	تِنْضَمّ	*btindámm*	بْتِنْضَمّ
ínti	*nḍammáyti*	نْضَمّيْتي	*tindámmi*	تِنْضَمّي	*btindámmi*	بْتِنْضَمّي
íntu	*nḍammáytu*	نْضَمّيْتوا	*tindámmu*	تِنْضَمّوا	*btindámmu*	بْتِنْضَمّوا
húwwi	*nḍamm*	نْضَمّ	*yindámm*	يِنْضَمّ	*byindámm*	بْيِنْضَمّ
híyyi	*nḍámmit*	نْضَمِّت	*tindámm*	تِنْضَمّ	*btindámm*	بْتِنْضَمّ
hínni	*nḍámmu*	نْضَمّوا	*yindámmu*	يِنْضَمّوا	*byindámmu*	بْيِنْضَمّوا

	imperative	
ínta	*nḍamm*	نْضَمّ
ínti	*nḍámmi*	نْضَمّي
íntu	*nḍámmu*	نْضَمّوا

	active participle	
masculine	*mindámm*	مِنْضَمّ
feminine	*mindámmi*	مِنْضَمّة
plural	*mindammīn*	مِنْضَمّين

نْضمّيْت لفريق كُرِة السّلِّة بِالجامْعة.

I joined the university's basketball team.

ما بِتْحِبّ تِنْضمّ معْنا عالطّاوْلِة؟

Wouldn't you like to join us at the table?

نْضمّي عَ هاي المجْموعة.

Join this group!

دايمْاً بِنْضمّ مع الضّعيف لقوّيه.

I always join the weak to make them stronger.

هَيْدول الجّماعة مِنْضمّين مع هَيْدا الحِزِب.

These people support this political party.

	perfect		imperfect		bi-imperfect	
ána	*naṭárit*	نَطَرِت	*únṭur*	أُنْطُر	*búnṭur*	بْنْطُر
níḥna	*naṭárna*	نَطَرْنا	*núnṭur*	نْنْطُر	*mnúnṭur*	مْنْنْطُر
ínta	*naṭárit*	نَطَرِت	*túnṭur*	تْنْطُر	*btúnṭur*	بْتْنْطُر
ínti	*naṭárti*	نَطَرْتي	*túnṭri*	تْنْطْري	*btúnṭri*	بْتْنْطْري
íntu	*naṭártu*	نَطَرْتوا	*túnṭru*	تْنْطْروا	*btúnṭru*	بْتْنْطْروا
húwwi	*náṭar*	نَطَر	*yúnṭur*	يْنْطُر	*byúnṭur*	بْيْنْطُر
híyyi	*náṭarit*	نَطَرِت	*túnṭur*	تْنْطُر	*btúnṭur*	بْتْنْطُر
hínni	*náṭaru*	نَطَروا	*yúnṭru*	يْنْطْروا	*byúnṭru*	بْيْنْطْروا

	imperative	
ínta	*nṭūr*	نْطور
ínti	*nṭuri*	نْطُري
íntu	*nṭuru*	نْطُروا

	active participle	
masculine	*nāṭir*	ناطِر
feminine	*nāṭra*	ناطْرَة
plural	*nāṭrīn*	ناطْرين

نطروا للسّاعة ٤ وما بيّنِت.

They waited until four, but you didn't show up.

لازِم تْنْطُر دَوْرك لَيِطْلع اِسْمك.

You should wait for your turn until you hear your name.

بْنْطُر مايْك كِلّ يوْم بْنفْس المحلّ.

I wait for Mike every day in the same place.

نْطور شْوَيّ صْغيرِة لتاخُد معك صحِن الحِلو لتيْتا إمّ نزيه.

Wait a little bit in order to take the plate of sweets with you to grandma Em Nazih.

منّا ناطْرين حدا يْدِلّنا عالطّريق.

We are not waiting for anybody to give us directions.

89 *hollow measure VII* **to be said** نْقال

	perfect		imperfect		bi-imperfect	
húwwi	*nʔāl*	نْقال	*yinʔāl*	يِنْقال	*byinʔāl*	بْيِنْقال
híyyi	*nʔālit*	نْقالِت	*tinʔāl*	تِنْقال	*btinʔāl*	بْتِنْقال
hínni	*nʔālu*	نْقالوا	*yinʔālu*	يِنْقالوا	*byinʔālu*	بْيِنْقالوا

	imperative
ínta	
ínti	
íntu	

active participle		
masculine	*minʔāl*	مِنْقال
feminine	*minʔāli*	مِنْقالِة
plural	*minʔālīn*	مِنْقالين

⚠ ① This verb is only used in the third person.
② Most passive verbs do not have imperative forms.

نْقال بِالأخْبار إنّو الطّقِس حِلْو.

It was said in news that the weather is nice.

عم يِنْقال عنّك ذكي.

It is being said that you are smart.

ما بْتِنْقال عنّا ولا كِلْمِة زْيادِة.

Nothing more can be said about her.

كِرْمال ما بْيِنْقالوا عنْكُن ضْعاف، دْرُسوا.

Study hard so that no one says that you are weak.

سْمِعِت إشْيا مِنْقالِة عنِّك كْتير حِلْوِة.

I've heard a lot of nice things about you.

to be canceled نْلَغى

	perfect		imperfect		bi-imperfect	
ána	*nlaɣēt*	نْلَغيْت	*ínliɣi*	إِنْلِغي	*bínliɣi*	بِنْلِغي
níḫna	*nlaɣáyna*	نْلَغيْنا	*nínliɣi*	نِنْلِغي	*mnínliɣi*	مْنِنْلِغي
ínta	*nlaɣēt*	نْلَغيْت	*tínliɣi*	تِنْلِغي	*btínliɣi*	بْتِنْلِغي
ínti	*nlaɣáyti*	نْلَغَيْتي	*tínliɣi*	تِنْلِغي	*btínliɣi*	بْتِنْلِغي
íntu	*nlaɣáytu*	نْلَغَيْتوا	*tínliɣu*	تِنْلِغوا	*btínliɣu*	بْتِنْلِغوا
húwwi	*nláɣa*	نْلَغى	*yínliɣi*	يِنْلِغي	*byínliɣi*	بْيِنْلِغي
híyyi	*nláɣit*	نْلَغِت	*tínliɣi*	تِنْلِغي	*btínliɣi*	بْتِنْلِغي
hínni	*nláɣu*	نْلَغوا	*yínliɣu*	يِنْلِغوا	*byínliɣu*	بْيِنْلِغوا

	imperative
ínta	
ínti	
íntu	

	active participle	
masculine	*mílɣi*	مِلْغي
feminine	*milɣíyyi*	مِلْغِيّة
plural	*milɣiyyīn*	مِلْغِيّين

① Although this verb is only used in the third person, hypothetical first- and second-person forms are shown to model the conjugation patterns for other defective measure VII verbs.
② Most passive verbs do not have imperative forms.

الماتْش نْلَغى لأنّ الطّقِس مِش مْنيح.
The [soccer] match was canceled due to bad weather.

كيف بْيِنْلِغوا اِشْتِراكات الكهْربا.
How can the electricity subscription be canceled?

بْتِعْتِقِد الاِجْتِماع رح يِنْلِغي؟
Do you think the meeting will be canceled?

إذا ما بْتِدْفع هلّق بْيِنْلِغي حْسابك.
If you don't pay now your account will be canceled.

ما خبّروك إنّو سهْرِة مْبارِح منّا مِلْغية!
No one told you that the party last night wasn't canceled!

91 *geminate measure VIII* **to be interested** هْتَمّ

	perfect		imperfect		bi-imperfect	
ána	*htammēt*	هْتَمّيْت	*ihtámm*	إِهْتَمّ	*bihtámm*	بِهْتَمّ
níḫna	*htammáyna*	هْتَمَّيْنا	*nihtámm*	نِهْتَمّ	*mnihtámm*	مْنِهْتَمّ
ínta	*htammēt*	هْتَمّيْت	*tihtámm*	تِهْتَمّ	*btihtámm*	بْتِهْتَمّ
ínti	*htammáyti*	هْتَمَّيْتي	*tihtámmi*	تِهْتَمّي	*btihtámmi*	بْتِهْتَمّي
íntu	*htammáytu*	هْتَمَّيْتوا	*tihtámmu*	تِهْتَمّوا	*btihtámmu*	بْتِهْتَمّوا
húwwi	*htamm*	هْتَمّ	*yihtámm*	يِهْتَمّ	*byihtámm*	بْيِهْتَمّ
híyyi	*htámmit*	هْتَمِّت	*tihtámm*	تِهْتَمّ	*btihtámm*	بْتِهْتَمّ
hínni	*htámmu*	هْتَمّوا	*yihtámmu*	يِهْتَمّوا	*byihtámmu*	بْيِهْتَمّوا

	imperative	
ínta	*htamm*	هْتَمّ
ínti	*htámmi*	هْتَمّي
íntu	*htámmu*	هْتَمّوا

	active participle	
masculine	*mihtámm*	مِهْتَمّ
feminine	*mihtámmi*	مِهْتَمِّة
plural	*mihtammīn*	مِهْتَمّين

هالمدرْسِة بْيِهْتمّوا كْتير بْطُلّابْن.

This school really takes care of their students.

رامي، هْتمّ بْإخْتك الصّْغيرِة.

Rami, take care of your little sister.

ما هْتمّيْت بْصحّْتك.

You didn't take care of your health.

كْتير مِهْتمِّة تِدْرُس إعْلام.

She is very interested in studying media [studies].

بْحِبّ إهْتمّ بِالزّريعة.

I love looking after plants.

sound measure I **to arrive** وُصِل

	perfect		imperfect		bi-imperfect	
ána	*wṣúlit*	وْصُلِت	*ūṣal*	أُوصَل	*būṣal*	بوصَل
níḩna	*wṣúlna*	وْصُلْنا	*nūṣal*	نوصَل	*mnūṣal*	مْنوصَل
ínta	*wṣúlit*	وْصُلِت	*tūṣal*	توصَل	*btūṣal*	بْتوصَل
ínti	*wṣúlti*	وْصُلْتي	*tūṣali*	توصَلي	*btūṣali*	بْتوصَلي
íntu	*wṣúltu*	وْصُلْتوا	*tūṣalu*	توصَلوا	*btūṣalu*	بْتوصَلوا
húwwi	*wúṣil*	وُصِل	*yūṣal*	يوصَل	*byūwṣal*	بْيوصَل
híyyi	*wúṣlit*	وُصْلِت	*tūṣal*	توصَل	*btūṣal*	بْتوصَل
hínni	*wúṣlu*	وُصْلوا	*yūṣalu*	يوصَلوا	*byūṣalu*	بْيوصَلوا

	imperative	
ínta	*wṣāl*	وْصال
ínti	*wṣáli*	وْصَلي
íntu	*wṣálu*	وْصَلوا

	active participle	
masculine	*wāṣil*	واصِل
feminine	*wāṣli*	واصْلة
plural	*wāṣlīn*	واصْلين

لمّا وُصِلِت لعِنْدو عالمحلّ كان مْسكّر.

When I arrived at his shop, it was closed.

بسّ أُصل عالكافيه بْتلْفِنْلك.

When I arrive at the coffee shop, I will call you.

ما وُصِل عَ طْرابْلُس بعْد؟

Didn't he arrive in Tripoli yet?

رتّْبوا الصّالوْن لأنّ واصْلين الضُّيوف بعْد ساعة.

Tidy up the living room because the guests are arriving in an hour.

بْيوصلوا الوْلاد عالمدْرسِة مْأخّرين شْوَيّ.

The children arrive at school quite late.

to promise وَعَد

	perfect		imperfect		bi-imperfect	
ána	*w3ádit*	وْعَدِت	*ū3id*	أُوعِد	*bū3id*	بوعِد
níђna	*w3ádna*	وْعَدْنا	*nū3id*	نوعِد	*mnū3id*	مْنوعِد
ínta	*w3ádit*	وْعَدِت	*tū3id*	توعِد	*btū3id*	بْتوعِد
ínti	*w3ádti*	وْعَدْتي	*tū3di*	توعْدي	*btū3di*	بْتوعْدي
íntu	*w3ádtu*	وْعَدْتوا	*tū3du*	توعْدوا	*btū3du*	بْتوعْدوا
húwwi	*wá3ad*	وَعَد	*yū3id*	يوعِد	*byū3id*	بْيوعِد
híyyi	*wá3adit*	وَعَدِت	*tū3id*	توعِد	*btū3id*	بْتوعِد
hínni	*wá3adu*	وَعَدوا	*yū3du*	يوعْدوا	*byū3du*	بْيوعْدوا

	imperative	
ínta	*w3ād*	وْعاد
ínti	*w3ídi*	وْعِدي
íntu	*w3ídu*	وْعِدوا

	active participle	
masculine	*wē3id*	واعِد
feminine	*wē3di*	واعْدِة
plural	*wē3dīn*	واعْدين

وْعدْتي ما تْشاغْبي بِالصفّ، وما لْتزمْتي.

You promised not to make trouble in class, but you did.

يا علي ما توعِد النّاس إذا إنْتَ منّك قدّا.

Ali, don't make promises to people if you can't keep them.

بوعْدك ما إتْأخّر عليْك المرّة الجايِة.

I promise you I won't be late next time.

وْعِدوا إنْكُن ما تْئذوا بعْض.

Promise that you will never hurt each other!

أحْمد واعِد بيّو يِشْترِي بطّيخة مِن سْبينّيس.

Ahmed promised his father to buy a watermelon from Spinneys.

to fall وِقِع

	perfect		imperfect		bi-imperfect	
ána	wʔí3it	وْقِعِت	ūʔa3	أُوقَع	būʔa3	بوقَع
níħna	wʔí3na	وْقِعْنا	nūʔa3	نوقَع	mnūʔa3	مْنوقَع
ínta	wʔí3it	وْقِعِت	tūʔa3	توقَع	btūʔa3	بْتوقَع
ínti	wʔí3ti	وْقِعْتي	tūʔa3i	توقَعي	btūʔa3i	بْتوقَعي
íntu	wʔí3tu	وْقِعْتوا	tūʔa3u	توقَعوا	btūʔa3u	بْتوقَعوا
húwwi	wíʔi3	وِقِع	yūʔa3	يوقَع	byūʔa3	بْيوقَع
híyyi	wíʔ3it	وِقْعِت	tūʔa3	توقَع	btūʔa3	بْتوقَع
hínni	wíʔ3u	وِقْعوا	yūʔa3u	يوقَعوا	byūʔa3u	بْيوقَعوا

	imperative	
ínta	wʔā3	وْقاع
ínti	wʔá3i	وْقَعي
íntu	wʔá3u	وْقَعوا

	active participle	
masculine	wēʔi3	واقِع
feminine	wēʔ3a	واقْعَة
plural	wēʔ3īn	واقْعين

وْقِعِت بْجورة ما كِنْت شايْفا حدّ معْبد باخوس بِبْعلْبك.

I fell in a hole I didn't see near the Temple of Bacchus in Baalbek.

نْتِبْهي ما توقعي إِنْتي وماشْيِة عالطّريق.

Be careful not to fall down while walking on the road.

بْتوقع إذا ما خلّيْت حدا يْعلّمك كيف تْسوق بِسِكْليتّ.

You will fall if you don't let anyone teach you how to ride a bicycle.

وِقْعِت عالدّرج وكسرِت إجْرا.

She fell on the stairs and broke her leg.

ما تْعيد زات الشّغْلِة أحْسن ما توقع بْنفس الغلط.

Do not repeat the same process, or else you'll fall into the same mistake.

sound measure I

to stand وِقِف

	perfect		imperfect		bi-imperfect	
ána	*wʔífit*	وْقِفِت	*ūʔaf*	أُوقَف	*būʔaf*	بوقَف
níḫna	*wʔífna*	وْقِفْنا	*nūʔaf*	نوقَف	*mnūʔaf*	مْنوقَف
ínta	*wʔífit*	وْقِفِت	*tūʔaf*	توقَف	*btūʔaf*	بْتوقَف
ínti	*wʔífti*	وْقِفْتي	*tūʔafi*	توقَفي	*btūʔafi*	بْتوقَفي
íntu	*wʔíftu*	وْقِفْتوا	*tūʔafu*	توقَفوا	*btūʔafu*	بْتوقَفوا
húwwi	*wíʔif*	وِقِف	*yūʔaf*	يوقَف	*byūʔaf*	بْيوقَف
híyyi	*wíʔfit*	وِقْفِت	*tūʔaf*	توقَف	*btūʔaf*	بْتوقَف
hínni	*wíʔfu*	وِقْفوا	*yūʔafu*	يوقَفوا	*byūʔafu*	بْيوقَفوا

	imperative	
ínta	*wʔāf*	وْقاف
ínti	*wʔáfi*	وْقَفي
íntu	*wʔáfu*	وْقَفوا

	active participle	
masculine	*wēʔif*	واقِف
feminine	*wēʔfi*	واقْفِة
plural	*wēʔfīn*	واقْفين

ليْش واقِف لْوَحْدك بِالعتْمِة؟

Why are you standing alone in the dark?

بْشوفِك بِتْحِبّي توقفي عالبلاكوْن كْتير.

I see you like to stand on the balcony a lot.

بوقف بِالشّارِع كِرْمال آخُد سيرْفيس.

I stand in the street in order to take a taxi.

وْقاف هونيك، بِتْلقّى وايفاي.

Stand there and you'll get a wifi signal.

وْقِفِت بِالصّفّ تاخُد اكْلاتي.

I stood in line to get my food.

to stop وَقَّف

	perfect		imperfect		bi-imperfect	
ána	wa??áfit	وَقَّفت	wá??if	وَقِّف	bwá??if	بْوَقِّف
níħna	wa??áfna	وَقَّفْنا	nwá??if	نْوَقِّف	minwá??if	مِنْوَقِّف
ínta	wa??áfit	وَقَّفت	twá??if	تْوَقِّف	bitwá??if	بِتْوَقِّف
ínti	wa??áfti	وَقَّفْتي	twá??fi	تْوَقّْفي	bitwá??fi	بِتْوَقّْفي
íntu	wa??áftu	وَقَّفْتوا	twá??fu	تْوَقّْفوا	bitwá??fu	بِتْوَقّْفوا
húwwi	wá??af	وَقَّف	ywá??if	يْوَقِّف	biwá??if	بيوَقِّف
híyyi	wá??afit	وَقَّفِت	twá??if	تْوَقِّف	bitwá??if	بِتْوَقِّف
hínni	wá??afu	وَقَّفوا	ywá??fu	يْوَقّْفوا	biwá??fu	بيوَقّْفوا

	imperative	
ínta	wá??if	وَقِّف
ínti	wá??fi	وَقّْفي
íntu	wá??fu	وَقّْفوا

	active participle	
masculine	mwá??if	مْوَقِّف
feminine	mwá??fi	مْوَقّْفة
plural	mwá??fīn	مْوَقّْفين

وَقّفِت لصُفّ السِّيّارة.

I stopped to park the car.

هُوِّ مْوَقِّف الدِّخّان مِن زمان.

He stopped smoking a while ago.

رح يْوَقّْفوا شرْب بعْد الحفْلِة.

They will stop drinking after the party.

وَقِّف عِنْدك ورْفاع إيديْك!

Stop there and raise your hands.

ما رح يْوَقِّف سبّ عالعالم.

He won't stop cursing at people.

to be born ولِد

	perfect		imperfect		bi-imperfect	
ána	*wlídit*	وْلِدِت	*ūlad*	أُولَد	*būlad*	بولَد
níђna	*wlídna*	وْلِدْنا	*nūlad*	نولَد	*mnūlad*	مْنولَد
ínta	*wlídit*	وْلِدِت	*tūlad*	تولَد	*btūlad*	بْتولَد
ínti	*wlídti*	وْلِدْتي	*tūladi*	تولَدي	*btūladi*	بْتولَدي
íntu	*wlídtu*	وْلِدْتوا	*tūladu*	تولَدوا	*btūladu*	بْتولَدوا
húwwi	*wílid*	وِلِد	*yūlad*	يولَد	*byūlad*	بْيولَد
híyyi	*wíldit*	وِلْدِت	*tūlad*	تولَد	*btūlad*	بْتولَد
hínni	*wíldu*	وِلْدوا	*yūladu*	يولَدوا	*byūladu*	بْيولَدوا

	imperative	
ínta	*wlūd*	وْلود
ínti	*wládi*	وْلَدي
íntu	*wládu*	وْلَدوا

	active participle	
masculine	*wēlid*	والِد
feminine	*wēldi*	والْدِة
plural	*wēldīn*	والْدين

أيمْتى وْلِدِت؟

When were you born?

وِلِد بالـ١٩٨٠.

He was born in 1980.

أيمْتى رح يولد الصّبْي؟

When will the child be born?

مظْبوط إنِّك وْلِدْتي بْأميرْكا؟

Is it true that you were actually born in America?

جينان بْتولد عَ بُكْرا الصُّبْح.

Jinan will be born tomorrow morning.

98 *prepositional phrase* **there to be** كان في

	perfect		imperfect		present	
positive	*kēn fī*	كان في	*ykūn fī*	يْكون في	*fī*	في
negative	*mā kēn fī*	ما كان في	*mā ykūn fī*	ما يْكون في	*mā fī*	ما في

⚠

① In prepositional phrases, the verb كان *kēn* is invariable, remaining in the third-person singular form.

② The present tense is expressed without using the bi-imperfect form بيكون *bikūn*.

③ This structure is used before an indefinite subject, as in the first example.

كان في بْسايْنِة قاعْدِة عالحفّة.

There was a cat sitting on the ledge. = A cat was sitting on the ledge.

ما كان في حليب بِالبرّاد عالصُّبْح.

There wasn't any milk in the refrigerator this morning.

ما بدّي يْكون في مشاكِل بينْ اهْلي.

I don't want (there to be) any problems between my parents.

ما حَيْكون في فُرص مِتِل هَيْدي.

There won't be any more opportunities like this.

في كْتير ناس بِالحفْلِة.

There are a lot of people at the party.

99 *prepositional phrase* to have كان عِنْدو

	perfect		imperfect		present	
ána	*kēn 3índi*	كان عِنْدي	*ykūn 3índi*	يْكون عِنْدي	*3índi*	عِنْدي
níђna	*kēn 3ínna*	كان عِنّا	*ykūn 3ínna*	يْكون عِنّا	*3ínna*	عِنّا
ínta	*kēn 3índak*	كان عِنْدَك	*ykūn 3índak*	يْكون عِنْدَك	*3índak*	عِنْدَك
ínti	*kēn 3índik*	كان عِنْدِك	*ykūn 3índik*	يْكون عِنْدِك	*3índik*	عِنْدِك
íntu	*kēn 3índkun*	كان عِنْدْكُن	*ykūn 3índkun*	يْكون عِنْدْكُن	*3índkun*	عِنْدْكُن
húwwi	*kēn 3índu*	كان عِنْدو	*ykūn 3índu*	يْكون عِنْدو	*3índu*	عِنْدو
híyyi	*kēn 3índa*	كان عِنْدا	*ykūn 3índa*	يْكونعِنْدا	*3índa*	عِنْدا
hínni	*kēn 3índun*	كان عِنْدُن	*ykūn 3índun*	يْكونعِنْدُن	*3índun*	عِنْدُن

① In prepositional phrases, the verb كان *kēn* is invariable, remaining in the third-person singular form.

② The present tense is expressed without using the bi-imperfect form بيكون *bikūn*.

③ There are three prepositional structures to express 'have'. This is the most common. ➲ Compare **T-100** and **T-101**.

كان عِنْدُن جْنيْنِة كْتير حِلْوِة.
They had a beautiful garden.

ما عِنْدو زيْت بِالمحلّ.
He doesn't have oil in his shop.

بْتِحِبّ يْكون عِنْدا سِيّارة.
She likes having a car.

ليْه ما بِدْكُن يْكون عِنْدْكُن بلْكوْن.
Why don't you want to have a balcony?

عِنّا إكْس بوكْس جْديدِة.
We have a new Xbox.

جِدّي كان عِنْدو سِتّ إخْوِة.
My grandfather had six brothers.

prepositional phrase to have كان إلو

	perfect		imperfect		present	
ána	*kēn íli*	كان إلي	*ykūn íli*	يْكون إلي	*íli*	إلي
níħna	*kēn ílna*	كان إلْنا	*ykūn ílna*	يْكون إلْنا	*ílna*	إلْنا
ínta	*kēn ílak*	كان إلَك	*ykūn ílak*	يْكون إلَك	*ílak*	إلَك
ínti	*kēn ílik*	كان إلِك	*ykūn ílik*	يْكون إلِك	*ílik*	إلِك
íntu	*kēn ílkun*	كان إلْكُن	*ykūn ílkun*	يْكون إلْكُن	*ílkun*	إلْكُن
húwwi	*kēn ílu*	كان إلو	*ykūn ílu*	يْكون إلو	*ílu*	إلو
híyyi	*kēn íla*	كان إلا	*ykūn íla*	يْكون إلا	*íla*	إلا
hínni	*kēn ílun*	كان إلُن	*ykūn ílun*	يْكون إلُن	*ílun*	إلُن

① This construction usually translates 'have', but also 'be (intended) for', and 'get'.

② In prepositional phrases, the verb كان *kēn* is invariable, remaining in the third-person singular form.

③ The present tense is expressed without using the bi-imperfect form بيكون *bikūn*.

هَيْدا البيْت رح يْكون إلك بسّ تِكْبر.

This house will be yours when you grow up.

حَيْكون إلا وَرْتِة مِن بيّا.

She will get an inheritance from her father.

ما بدّي يْكون إلي هَيْدا اللوْن.

I don't want to have this color.

في إلْكُن أحْلى هْدية.

You will get an awesome gift.

101 *prepositional phrase* to have كان معو

	perfect		imperfect		present	
ána	*kēn má3i*	كان معي	*ykūn má3i*	يْكون معي	*má3i*	معي
níħna	*kēn má3na*	كان معْنا	*ykūn má3na*	يْكون معْنا	*má3na*	معْنا
ínta	*kēn má3ak*	كان معك	*ykūn má3ak*	يْكون معك	*má3ak*	معك
ínti	*kēn má3ik*	كان معِك	*ykūn má3ik*	يْكون معِك	*má3ik*	معِك
íntu	*kēn má3kun*	كان معْكُن	*ykūn má3kun*	يْكون معْكُن	*má3kun*	معْكُن
húwwi	*kēn má3u*	كان معو	*ykūn má3u*	يْكون معو	*má3u*	معو
híyyi	*kēn má3a*	كان معا	*ykūn má3a*	يْكون معا	*má3a*	معا
hínni	*kēn má3un*	كان معُن	*ykūn má3un*	يْكون معُن	*má3un*	معُن

① 'to have on oneself'
② In prepositional phrases, the verb كان *kēn* is invariable, remaining in the third-person singular form.
③ The present tense is expressed without using the bi-imperfect form بيكون *bikūn*.

كان معو الكُتُب بسّ ضيّعُن.
He had the books, but he lost them.

معْكُن مصاري؟
Do you have any money on you?

معي قلم إذا كِنْت بْعازْتو.
I have a pen if you need it.

كان معُن دْروس البيْت يْحِلّوهُن بْعُطْلِة الرّبيع.
They had homework to do during the spring holiday.

ما معك برّايِة؟
You don't have a pencil sharpener, do you?

102 *prepositional phrase* **to want** كان بَدّو

	perfect		imperfect		present	
ána	*kēn báddi*	كان بَدّي	*ykūn báddi*	يْكون بَدّي	*báddi*	بَدّي
níḫna	*kēn báddna*	كان بَدّْنا	*ykūn báddna*	يْكون بَدّْنا	*báddna*	بَدّْنا
	kēn bánna	كان بَنّا	*ykūn bánna*	يْكون بَنّا	*bánna*	بَنّا
ínta	*kēn báddak*	كان بَدَّك	*ykūn báddak*	يْكون بَدَّك	*báddak*	بَدَّك
ínti	*kēn báddik*	كان بَدِّك	*ykūn báddik*	يْكون بَدِّك	*báddik*	بَدِّك
íntu	*kēn báddkun*	كان بَدّْكُن	*ykūn báddkun*	يْكون بَدّْكُن	*báddkun*	بَدّْكُن
húwwi	*kēn báddu*	كان بَدّو	*ykūn báddu*	يْكون بَدّو	*báddu*	بَدّو
híyyi	*kēn bádda*	كان بَدّا	*ykūn bádda*	يْكون بَدّا	*bádda*	بَدّا
hínni	*kēn báddun*	كان بَدُّن	*ykūn báddun*	يْكون بَدُّن	*báddun*	بَدُّن

① بَدّ *badd-* is also commonly pronounced بِدّ *bidd-*.

② Notice the shortened form بَنّا *bánna* (common in relaxed speech), in which the *d* assimilates into *n*.

③ In prepositional phrases, the verb كان *kēn* is invariable, remaining in the third-person singular form.

④ The present tense is expressed without using the bi-imperfect بيكون *bikūn*.

ما كان بدّا تْغيرِّ اِخْتِصاصا.

She didn't want to change her major.

كان بدّْكُن تْغيرّْوا عفْش البيْت. شو صار!؟

You wanted to change the house decor. What happened?!

ليْه بدّْكُن تِترْكوا الجّامْعة؟

Why do you want to drop out of college?

بَدّك تِلْعب بِالطّابِة مع رِفْقاتك؟

Do you want to play football with your friends?

بْنْجور، بَدّي إحْجُز أوْضة بِالأوْتيل. قدّيْه بِتْريد؟

Hello! I want to reserve a room in the hotel. How much would it cost? [lit. How much do you want?]

رح يْكون بدّو إيصال الفاتورة.

He will want the receipt for the bill.

103 *prepositional phrase* **to be able to** كان فِيو

	perfect		imperfect		present	
ána	*kēn fīni*	كان فيني	*ykūn fīni*	يْكون فيني	*fīni*	فيني
	kēn fíyi	كان فِيي	*ykūn fíyi*	يْكون فِيي	*fíyi*	فِيي
níḫna	*kēn fīna*	كان فينا	*ykūn fīna*	يْكون فينا	*fīna*	فينا
ínta	*kēn fīk*	كان فيك	*ykūn fīk*	يْكون فيك	*fīk*	فيك
ínti	*kēn fīki*	كان فيكي	*ykūn fīki*	يْكون فيكي	*fīki*	فيكي
íntu	*kēn fīkun*	كان فيكُن	*ykūn fīkun*	يْكون فيكُن	*fīkun*	فيكُن
húwwi	*kēn fíyu*	كان فِيو	*ykūn fíyu*	يْكون فِيو	*fíyu*	فِيو
híyyi	*kēn fíya*	كان فِيا	*ykūn fíya*	يْكون فِيا	*fíya*	فِيا
hínni	*kēn fíyun*	كان فِيُن	*ykūn fíyun*	يْكون فِيُن	*fíyun*	فِيُن

① Notice that here are two *ána* forms, both of which are common.
② In prepositional phrases, the verb كان *kēn* is invariable, remaining in the third-person singular form.

③ The present tense is expressed without using the bi-imperfect بيكون *bikūn*.
④ Compare with قِدِر *ʔídir* in **T-73**.

كان فِيو يِتِّصِل عالموْبايْل.
He could have called by mobile phone.

ما فيكي تْجيبي بْطريقِك الكنْزِة؟
Can't you bring the sweater with you?

فيني غنّي معك عالمسْرح؟
Can I sing with you on stage?

فِيُن يْركّْبوا بانِرْز عالطُّرْقات.
They can put the banners on the streets.

كان فينا نِنْهي المَوْضوع كِرْمال ما يْصير مشاكِل.
We could have put an end to the matter
so that there wouldn't be problems.

ersonal Pronouns

ndependent Pronouns

evantine Arabic has eight persons, which means there are eight pronouns and ight conjugations for each tense. The following table shows the eight ndependent pronouns, that is, pronouns which are independent words, and not refixes or suffixes.

	LCA	English	
ána	أَنا	I	*first-person masculine/feminine singular*
níħna	نِحْنا	we	*first-person masculine/feminine dual/plural*
ínta	إِنْتَ	you	*second-person masculine singular*
ínti	إِنْتي	you	*second-person feminine singular*
íntu	إِنْتو	you (guys)	*second-person masculine/feminine dual/plural*
húwwi	هُوِّ	he; it	*third-person masculine singular*
híyyi	هِيِّ	she; it	*third-person feminine singular*
hínni	هِنِّ	they	*third-person masculine/feminine dual/plural*

Compared to Modern Standard Arabic, Levantine olloquial Arabic has four fewer pronouns, as the ual is absorbed into the plural, which is used for oth genders.

LCA	MSA
إِنْتو	أَنْتُما / أَنْتُمْ / أَنْتُنَّ
هِنِّ	هُما / هُمْ / هُنَّ

You can hear the pronunciation of the independent pronouns on audio track 6B (**T-76B**).

eep in mind that a conjugated verb contains a prefix and/or suffix which pecifies the subject of the verb, so subject pronouns are not usually necessary. ndependent pronouns are only used before conjugated verbs to emphasize the ubject. Compare the following:

bħíbbak.	بْحِبَّك.	I love you.
<u>ána</u> baħíbbak.	أنا بْحِبَّك.	<u>I</u> love you.

Although independent pronouns usually refer to the subject of a verb, they ca
also be used to emphasize the object when following an object pronoun suffix.

bħíbbak <u>ínta</u>.	بْحِبّك إِنْتَ.	I love **<u>you</u>**.

Independent pronouns are more commonly used in the absence of a conjugate verb: in isolation, before active participles, and in sentences without a verb. (Th verb *to be* is not normally expressed in the present tense in Arabic. ➲ **T-76B**)

mīn? <u>ána</u>?	مين؟ أنا؟	Who? Me?
<u>húwwi</u> lāzim yēkul.	هُوِّ لازِم ياكُل.	He must eat.
<u>híyyi</u> ktīr jamīli.	هِيِّ كْتير جميلِة.	She is very beautiful.

Suffixed Pronouns

Subject Pronoun Suffixes

There are two sets of subject pronoun suffixes. One is used in conjugations of th perfect tense (➲ **The Perfect Tense** *p. 107*), while the other is used for other th imperfect. (➲ **The Imperfect Tense** *p. 108*).

Direct Object Pronoun Suffixes

Object pronoun suffixes are attached to conjugated verbs. The form some tak depends on whether the verb ends in a consonant (**C**) or vowel (**V**).

šēf	شاف	he saw
šēf<u>ni</u>.	شافْني.	He saw me.
šēf<u>u</u>.	شافو.	He saw it.
lēʔa	لاقى	he found
lēʔāni.	لاقاني.	He found me.
lēʔā.	لاقاه.	He found it.

persons	C+		V+	
ána	*-ni*	ـني	*-ni*	ني
níħna	*-na*	ـنا	*-na*	نا
ínta	*-ak*	ـَك	*-k*[2]	ك
ínti	*-ik*	ـِك	*-ki*	كي
íntu	*-kun*	ـكُن	*-kun*	كُن
húwwi	*-u*	ـو[1]	-[2]	ه
híyyi	*-a*	ـا[3]	*-(h/w/y)a*[4]	ا
hínni	*-un*	ـُن[3]	*-(h/w/y)un*[4]	ن

[1] also commonly spelled ـهُ
[2] preceding vowel is lengthened
[3] also commonly spelled ـها and ـهُن; sometimes pronounced *-ha* and *-hun* in careful speech
[4] a buffer consonant is inserted in pronunciation, *h* after *a/ā* (usually written), *w* after *u/ū*, *y* after *i/ī*

direct Object Pronoun Suffixes

ána	*-li*	ـلي
níħna	*-lna*	ـلْنا
ínta	*-lak*	ـلَك
ínti	*-lik*	ـلِك
íntu	*-lkun*	ـلْكُن
húwwi	*-lu*	ـلو
híyyi	*-la*	ـلا
hínni	*-lun*	ـلُن

Indirect object pronouns are suffixed onto the preposition لـ *la-*, which, in turn, are commonly suffixed onto the verb they complement.

kátab	كتب	he wrote
kátabli.	كتبْلي.	He wrote to me.
katabnālu risēli.	كتبْنالو رِسالِة.	We wrote him a letter.

erb Forms and Uses

he Base Form

he base form is the most basic form of a verb, free of any prefixes or suffixes. In oth Arabic and English, the base form is the form of a verb listed in dictionary ntries. In English, this is the infinitive (*be, go, have, etc.*). In Arabic, the base form the third-person masculine singular (*húwwi*) of the perfect tense. So, although e verb راح *rāħ*, for example, might literally mean *'he went'* in a sentence, when ted in isolation, its translation would be *go* or *to go*, the infinitive.

he Perfect Tense

rm

he *húwwi* form, as mentioned above, is the base rm. It has no suffix. Other persons are conjugated by e addition of a suffix to this base form, as shown in is table.

a first- or second-person conjugation, the word ress shifts to the syllable directly before the suffix.

t's take a look at the perfect tense suffixes on the erb درس *dáras* ('to study') on the next page:

ána	*-it*	ـِت
níħna	*-na*	ـْنا
ínta	*-it*	ـِت
ínti	*-ti*	ـْتي
íntu	*-tu*	ـْتوا
húwwi	-	
híyyi	*-it*	ـِت
hínni	*-u*	ـوا

	perfect	
ána	*darás<u>it</u>*	دَرَسِت
níḫna	*darás<u>na</u>*	دَرَسْنا
ínta	*darás<u>it</u>*	دَرَسِت
ínti	*darás<u>ti</u>*	دَرَسْتي
íntu	*darás<u>tu</u>*	دَرَسْتوا
húwwi	*dáras*	دَرَس
híyyi	*dáras<u>it</u>*	دَرَسِت
hínni	*dáras<u>u</u>*	دَرَسوا

Notice that the *ána* and *ínta* forms are identical, but context usually eliminates ambiguity. The *híyyi* form is also written identically but stressed differently.*

When the base form ends in ن *n*, the ensuing double consonant is written with a shadda (ّ◌) in the Arabic script:

sákan	سكن	he lived
sakánna	كتبْلي.	we lived

Use

The perfect tense specifies that the action is finished. It is equivalent to the simple past and present perfect tenses of English.

katábit rrisēli mbēriḫ.	كتبِت الرِّسالِة مْبارِح.	*I <u>wrote</u> the letter yesterday.*
kínna hunēk marrtēn.	كِنّا هُنيْك مرّْتين.	*We <u>have been</u> there twice.*

The Imperfect Tense

Form

While the perfect tense is conjugated using suffixes, the imperfect tense uses prefixes. Three persons additionally add suffixes. The prefixes shown here contain the vowel *kasra* (ِ◌ *i*), although, with a quick look through the tables in this book, you will see that there are variations, depending on the verb, such as replacing *kasra* with *Damma* (ُ◌ *u*) or *sukuun* (ْ◌ no vowel**).

The imperfect prefixes and suffixes are not added to the base form but an imperfect stem.

ána	*i-*	إِ
níḫna	*ni-*	نِـ
ínta	*ti-*	تِـ
ínti	*ti- -i*	تِـي
íntu	*ti- -u*	تِـوا
húwwi	*yi-*	يِـ
híyyi	*ti-*	تِـ
hínni	*yi- -u*	يِـوا

* In defective verbs, the *híyyi* form differs from the *ána/ínta* form.
***In the case of the ána form, this means there is no prefix.*

imperfect		
ána	i̱drus	إِدْرُس
níħna	ni̱drus	نِدْرُس
ínta	ti̱drus	تِدْرُس
ínti	ti̱dirsi̱	تدِرْسي
íntu	ti̱dirsu̱	تدِرْسوا
húwwi	yi̱drus	يِدْرُس
híyyi	ti̱drus	تِدْرُس
hínni	yi̱dirsu̱	يدِرْسوا

Use

The imperfect tense* has several uses.

① The imperfect can follow an *auxiliary*. An auxiliary can be an active participle, conjugated verb, or other certain types of words. The equivalent in English is modal verbs and others than can precede a second verb (which is infinitive or gerund). For example, *can go, want to eat, like dancing*. In these examples, *can, want,* and *like* function as auxiliaries, while the underlined verbs would be translated with the imperfect in Levantine Arabic.

fíyyu yídrus.	فيّو يِدْرُس.	He can study.
bádda tídrus.	بدّا تِدْرُس.	She wants to study.
minħíbb nídrus.	مِنْحِبّ نِدْرُس.	We like studying.

Examples of auxiliaries used with the imperfect can be seen in the example sentences throughout the book. The imperfect can sometimes be replaced with a verbal noun (مصْدر) after an auxiliary.

báddi ɣáyyir ixtiṣāṣi.	بدّي غيِّر إخْتصاصي.	I want to change my major.
báddi taɣyīr ixtiṣāṣi.	بدّي تغْيير إخْتصاصي.	I want to change my major.

② The imperfect is used to express the future when preceded by the particle رح *raħ* or the prefixed particle حـ *ħa-*.

future	positive		negative	
	raħ	رح	mā ħa-	ما حـ
less common	ħa-	حـ	mā raħ	ما رح

raħ íktub risēli.	رح إكْتُب رِسالِة.	I will write a letter.
mā ħa-íktub risēli.	ما حإكْتُب رِسالِة.	I won't write a letter.

---

* also referred to as the *bare imperfect* in order to differentiate it from the *bi-imperfect*

③ The imperfect follows the progressive particle عم *3am*, equivalent to the present continuous tense of English. It refers to actions happening at the time of speaking, as well as those that are repetitive or ongoing.

3an šū <u>3am</u> tíɦki?	عن شو عم تِحْكي؟	What are you talking about?
3áli <u>3am</u> yjámmi3 maṣariyyātu.	علي عم يْجمّع مصريّاتو.	Ali is saving up his money.

عم *3am* need not be repeated in a string of verbs.

<u>3am</u> tútbux u tíɦdar tilfizyõ.	عم تُطْبُخ وتِحْضر تِلْفزْيون.	She's cooking and watching TV.

The negative particle ما *mā* precedes عم *3am.*

<u>mā 3am</u> íɦdar film.	ما عم إحْضر فيلْم.	I'm not watching a movie.

④ A negative imperative (command) is expressed by placing ما *mā* in front of a second-person imperfect verb.

<u>mā</u> tídʔar fíyyi.	ما تِدْقر فيي.	Don't touch me.
<u>mā</u> trūɦi la-wáɦdik la-hunēk.	ما تْروحي لَوَحْدِك لَهُنيْك.	Don't go there alone.

⑤ An imperfect verb follows certain conjunctions of purpose* and time**.

rāɦit 3a-lbáɦir <u>ta</u>-tísbaɦ.	راحِت عالبحِر تَتِسْبح.	She went to the beach <u>(in order) to</u> swim.
3am bídrus <u>kirmēl</u> mā -sʔuṭ.	عم بِدْرُس كِرْمال ما إسقُط.	I'm studying <u>so that</u> I don't fail.
fátaɦ ššibbēk ʔábil mā ynēm.	فتح الشُّبّاك قبِل ما يْنام.	He opened the window <u>before</u> he went to bed.

* تَ *ta-*, لَ *la-*, حتّى *ɦátta*, عشان *3ašān*, مِنْشان *minšān*, كِرْمال *kirmēl* 'in order to', 'so that'
** قبِل ما *ʔábil mā* 'before'; بعِد ما *bá3id mā* 'after'; بسّ *bass* 'when'

The Bi-Imperfect Tense

Form

The bi-imperfect is formed by prefixing ب to conjugations in the imperfect tense. If the imperfect prefix has a vowel, the bi-imperfect prefix takes a sukuun (ْ no vowel). If it has a sukuun, the bi-imperfect prefix takes a kasra (ِ i). The *níɦn* form takes م (m) instead of ب (b).

ána	*bi-*	بِـ
níħna	*<u>m</u>ni-*	مْنِـ
ínta	*bti-*	بْتِـ
ínti	*bti- -i*	بْتِـي
íntu	*bti- -u*	بْتِـوا
húwwi	*byi-*	بْيِـ
híyyi	*bti-*	بْتِـ
hínni	*byi- -u*	بْيِـوا

tídrus → *<u>b</u>tídrus* تِدْرُس ← بْتِدْرُس
tsákkir → *<u>bi</u>tsákkir* تْسكِّر ← بِتْسكِّر
yídrus → *<u>b</u>yídrus* يِدْرُس ← بْيِدْرُس
ysákkir → *<u>bi</u>(y)sákkir* يْسكِّر ← بيسكِّر

otice that, in the last example above, *biy-* is nearly ways pronounced *bi-* in relaxed pronunciation.

se

) The bi-imperfect tense most often corresponds) the present simple tense of English, referring to eneral truths and habits.

bi-l3ādi bfīʔ mitʔáxxar. بِالعادِة بْفيق متأخِّر. I usually get up late.
btíħki 3árabi? بْتِحْكي عربي؟ Do you speak Arabic?

is used in announcements: I promise..., I congratulate..., I swear...

bū3adak mā -nsāk. بوعدك ما إنْساك. I promise not to forget you.

) The bi-imperfect can also refer to future, especially to convey intentions.

bass ūṣal btálfinlak. بسّ أوصل بْتلْفِنْلك. When I arrive, I'll call you.

The progressive particle عم *3am* is usually followed by a bare imperfect verb, ut can, less commonly, precede a bi-imperfect verb.

The bi-imperfect is sometimes interchangeable with the imperfect. Their uses ay vary among native speakers, not only from region to region but within Beirut, well.

gative: The negative of all tenses is formed by adding ما *mā* before the verb (and ny future or progressive particle).

The previous sections lay out the most common uses of the perfect, imperfect, nd bi-imperfect tenses of Levantine Arabic. Keep in mind that Levantine verb nses will not always correlate directly with those of English. As you read xample sentences throughout this book, you will develop a better nderstanding of the tenses' uses.

The Imperative

Form

The imperative is based on the imperfect tense. The positive imperative is forme by removing the personal prefix تْـ *t-* or تِـ *ti-*.

tsákkir → sákkir	تْسكّر ← سكّر
tnēmi → nēmi	تْنامي ← نامي
tírmu → rmū	تِرْموا ← رْموا

For sound measure I verbs (➲ **Verb Patterns** *p. 115*), the pattern is a bit differen The masculine imperative takes a long vowel, while the feminine and plural form have short vowels. The voweling is not always predictable and should be learne for each verb.

ktūb	كْتوب
ktíbi	كْتِبي
ktíbu	كْتِبوا

A couple of verbs have irregular positive imperative forms. The negative form however, are regular. (➲ **T-1**, **T-42**)

Negative: The negative imperative is always the same as the negative imperfec that is, an imperfect verb preceded by ما *ma*. (➲ **The Imperfect Tense** ④ *p. 110*

Use

Imperatives are used to give the listener a command to do something.

tá3a la-hūn!	تعا لهون!	Come here!
mšī b3īd 3ánni!	مْشي بْعيد عنّي!	Get away from me!
mā tá3mlu hēk!	ما تَعْمْلوا هيْك!	Don't do ح that!

he Active Participle

orm

ne active participle is, grammatically, an adjective derived from a verb. As an djective, it reflects the gender and number of its subject but is not conjugated or person as a verb would be. The active participle therefore only has three orms: masculine, feminine, and plural. A subject pronoun can precede the active articiple to specify person when necessary.

n adjective is made feminine by adding ـِة -*i* or ـَة -*a* to the masculine form. The ronunciation of ـة depends largely on the preceding consonant*. The plural uffix is ـين -*īn*. The table below shows the active participle forms for the verb عِمِل *'mil 'to do'*, a measure I verb. Notice the pattern: the first consonant is followed y ـا -*ē***. The second consonant is followed by *'kasra'* (ـِ *i*), which elides (is mitted) in the feminine and plural forms.

	active participle	
masculine	*lēbis*	لابِس
feminine	*lēbsi*	لابْسِة
plural	*lēbsīn*	لابْسين

*The feminine suffix is pronounced -*a* after ض *d̦*, ص *ṣ*, ط *ț*, ظ *z̦*, ع *3*, ح *ḩ*, and ر *r*.
**The long vowel of the first syllable is pronounced *ā* after ض *d̦*, ص *ṣ*, ط *ț*, ظ *z̦*, and sometimes ع *3*, ح *ḩ* and ر *r*.

on-measure I verbs have a different pattern, taking the prefix مـُ *m-* (or مِـ *mi-*). ake a look at the active participles in the tables throughout this book to see xamples.

:gative: As the active participle is somewhat of a verb and adjective at the same me, it can be made negative with ما *ma* (as verbs are), مِش *miš* (as nominal redicates are), or even a negative pronoun (➲ **T-76**[B]).

ána mā rāyiḩ	أنا ما رايِح	I'm not going
ána miš rāyiḩ	أنا مِش رايِح	I'm not going
mánni rāyiḩ	منّي رايِح	I'm not going

;e

ne active participle has several uses. It is sometimes interchangeable with other nses to express the past, present, and future. As its usage is highly idiomatic, in addition to reading the various uses listed below, look for the active participle in examples throughout this book to gain a better understanding of its natural usage.

① Verbs of motion and location are expressed with an active participle (rather than عم *3am* + imperfect verb) when the action is happening at the moment of speaking.

ána rāyiḫ أنا رايح I'm going

② The active participle can express the future.

šū 3āmil bi-ssáhra? شو عامِل بالسّهْرة؟ What are you doing tonight?
mballšīn šɣil bakkīr. مْبلّشين شِغِل بكّير. They will begin work early.

③ The active participle is commonly used with verbs of mental state (know, remember, understand, feel, etc.).

ḫāsis ḫāli mnīḫ. حاسِس حالي مْنيح. I feel good.
miš mitzákkar. مِش مِتْزكّر. I don't remember.

④ With verbs (except those of motion, location, or mental state), the active participle can express a past action, often with a present result, equivalent to the present perfect tense of English.

šū mit3állam bi-jjām3a? شو مِتْعلّم بِالجّامْعة؟ What did you study in college?
ʔēryi kill riwayātu. قارْيِة كِلّ رِواياتو. She has read all of his novels.

⚠ The passive participle also exists in Levantine Arabic. Although it is formed from verbs, its use is strictly as an adjective, and therefore beyond the scope of this book.

Compound Tenses

Compound tenses are created by following كان *kēn* 'to be' with a perfect or imperfect verb, or active participle. The most common combinations (with كان *kēn* in the perfect tense) are shown in the table below, using the verb عِمِل *3ímil 'to do'* as an example.

compound tenses			
+ perfect verb	kēn 3ímil	كان عِمِل	he had done
+ imperfect verb	kēn yá3mil	كان يَعْمِل	he used to do he was doing
+ continuous particle	kēn 3am yá3mil	كان عم يَعْمِل	he was doing
+ future particle	kēn raħ yá3mil	كان رح يَعْمِل	he was going to do
+ active participle	kēn 3āmil	كان عامِل	he was doing he used to do

ɔth verbs are conjugated to agree with their subject.

<u>kēnu xállaṣu</u> drūsun lámma wuṣílit.	كانوا خلّصوا دْروسْن لمّا وُصِلِت.	They had [already] finished their homework when I arrived.
<u>kēnit tnēm</u> btáxit báyya u ímma.	كانِت تْنام بْتخِت بيّا وإمّا.	She used to sleep in her parents' bed.
<u>kíntu 3am</u> tēklu?	كِنْتوا عم تاكْلوا؟	Were you eating?
<u>kēn raħ yílbus</u> ṭá2im.	كان رح يِلْبُس طقِم.	He was going to wear a suit.
<u>kínna rāyħīn</u> 3a-ššíɣil, ...	كِنّا رايْحين عالشّغِل، ...	They were going [on their way] to work when...

erb Patterns

easures

you have studied Modern Standard or Classical Arabic, you will already be miliar with verb measures, sometimes called forms (in Arabic: أَوْزان). Levantine ·abic, and other dialects of Arabic, also build verbs according to patterns rouped into these so-called 'measures'). While it is not necessary to understand ·rb measures in order to conjugate and use Levantine Arabic verbs, being aware them will help you identify commonalities among verbs—patterns that will ·lp you memorize, internalize, and be able to reproduce correctly conjugated ·rbs more easily.

·abic verbs are based on *roots,* which consist of three, and sometimes four, ɔnsonants (called *radicals*). Radicals are then put into patterns (measures) to rm actual words. Verbs of different measures may share a common root and ive a related meaning. For example, the root و ق ف is used in measure I to form e verb وِقِف *wíʔif* (*'to* stand') and in measure II to form the verb وَقّف *wáʔʔaf* (*'to stop'*). Both verbs share the same root and a related meaning, namely 'lack c motion'. Measure I verbs, like وِقِف *wíʔif*, have short vowels but no other addition to the radicals. Measure II verbs double the second radical, ق *ʔ*, in the exampl above. Other measures have their own distinctive patterns.

Following is a rundown of the measures and how they differ from each othe using the base form. Tables are referenced as examples.

Measure I verbs are simply the three radicals separated by two short vowel Because there are several combinations of vowels used in the perfect an imperfect forms, measure I verbs are subdivided using numbers. ➲ *p. 118*

Measure II verbs double the second radical, which is followed by ◌َ *a* in the perfe and ◌ِ *i* in the imperfect. ➲ *p. 125*

Measure III verbs have the long vowel ـا *-ē/-ā* after the first radical. The secon radical is followed by ◌َ *a* in the perfect and ◌ِ *i* in the imperfect. ➲ *p. 128*

Measure IV verbs begin with أ *ʔa-* in the perfect tense. This form is rather rar limited to a few borrowings from Modern Standard Arabic. ➲ *p. 129*

Measure V verbs are similar to measure II verbs, having a doubled second radica However, they also take the prefix تْ *t-*. The second radical is followed by ◌َ *a* i both the perfect and imperfect tenses. They are usually, but not alway intransitive, and can also be used as the passive of transitive measure II verb ➲ *p. 129*

Measure VI verbs are to measure III verbs as measure V verbs are to measure verbs. They resemble measure III verbs, but like measure V verbs, they take th prefix تْ *t-*. ➲ *p. 130*

Measure VII verbs are used as the passive of measure I verbs. They begin wit the prefix نْ *n-*. However, unlike measure I verbs, there is a single vowel patter for measure VII verbs. That is, verbs of different subcategories of measure I wi have an identical vowel pattern in the passive. ➲ *p. 130*

Measure XIII verbs insert a ت *-t-* after the first radical. ➲ *p. 131*

Measure IX verbs take *'sukuun'* (◌ْ no vowel) on the first radical and double th third radical. ➲ *p. 131*

easure X verbs begin with the prefix ستـ *sta-*. ➲ *p. 132*

easure XI verbs consist of four radicals. ➲ *p. 132*

ualities

ound verbs have three radicals, none of which are identical. Also, neither the cond nor third radical is و *w* or ي *y*.

e letters و *w* and ي *y* are known as *weak radicals.* They turn into vowels (and in me positions even disappear from writing when pronounced as short vowels) certain measures and positions.

ollow verbs have و *w* or ي *y* as the second radical, which becomes a long *ā* in the ase form of certain measures, leaving only two radicals as consonants. The *ā* is ortened in first- and second-person perfect conjugations, and it may change to other long vowel in the imperfect.

efective verbs have و *w* or ي *y* as the third radical, which is treated as a vowel. It short in the base form, lengthened or replaced in certain conjugations.

eminate verbs have the same consonant for the second and third radicals, hich remain adjacent to each other as a double consonant. This causes geminate rbs to have different conjugation patterns than sound verbs do.

regular verbs: A handful of verbs do not fit into any of the measures. They quire special attention.

Indexes

750 verbs are listed in the indexes, by pattern, alphabetically in Arabic, and b
English translation. The pattern for each verb is designated by an alphanumer
indicator (1s1, 8d, etc.) Verbs which have their own tables are shown in bold an
their table numbers are preceded by **T-**.

Index by Table Pattern

The tables in this book show the conjugations for dozens of the most common
used verbs in Levantine Arabic, but, at the same time, the patterns in these table
can be applied to other verbs with identical or nearly identical patterns, allowir
you to conjugate nearly any verb in the language. This index arranges verbs int
groups with common conjugation patterns.

1s1 *sound measure* / ①

بحش dig
بخع humiliate
بعت send; mail
بلع swallow
تبع follow
جرح wound, injure, hurt
جمع add, add up; harvest
حصل obtain على
خدع deceive
خلع snatch
دعس step
دعس tread on على
T-32 **دفع** pay
T-33 **دقر** touch
دهن paint
رفع raise
زحط slip
زرع plant (a seed), grow (a plant)
زعب kick; speak harshly
T-42 **سأل** ask
سبح swim
سحب withdraw
سمح allow, permit
شحد beg (for money)
شرح explain
شلح undress; take off, remove
صنع manufacture
ضهر leave; go out
طبع print
طحن grind
طرح subtract
ظهر appear
T-66 **فتح** open
فحص examine
فقس click on على
فلح plow (field); work hard
T-71 **قبض** earn
قنع convince

	كبر	grow (up); get big
	كسب	win, gain, acquire
	لحس	lick
	لقط	catch
	لمع	shine
	مدح	praise
	مزح	joke; kid
	مسح	wipe, mop
	منع	forbid
	نجح	succeed
	نزع	spoil, ruin *(tr.)*
	نسخ	copy
	نصح	advise

1s2 *sound measure I* ②

	برد	file (down)
	برد	get cold
	برز	become clear
	برش	grate
	برش	grate
T-7	**برم**	turn (around); visit, roam
	بزق	spit
T-10	**ترك**	leave; quit
	تهم	accuse
	جبر	forc
	جذب	attract
	جلف	scratch
	حبس	imprison
	حجز	book, reserve
	حرث	plow
	حرس	guard
	حرق	burn
	حرم	deprive
	حسب	calculate
	حكم	govern
	حلب	milk
	حلف	swear
	حلق	shave
	خبز	bake
	ختم	conclude, finish; stamp
	خدم	serve
	خلق	create
T-31	**درس**	study
	دفش	push, shove
	دفن	bury
	دلق	pour
	ذكر	mention
	رزق	(God) bless
	رسم	draw
	رقص	dance
	ركض	run
	رمز	represent, symbolize
	سرق	steal
	سعل	cough
	سفق	hit, strike; slam
	سقط	fail
	سكت	be quiet, shut up
T-46	**سكن**	live
	سلق	boil (food)
	سند	support

	شرق	(sun) rise
	شطف	rinse
	شعر	feel بِـ
	شقل	lift and carry
T-52	**شكر**	thank
	شمل	include
	صبغ	dye one's hair
	صرف	spend (money); change (money); fire, dismiss (from a job)
	ضرب	hit, beat; multiply
	طرد	fire
T-57	**طلب**	request, order
	عبس	frown, knit one's brow, scowl
	عجب	please, appeal to
	عذر	excuse
	عزف	play (instrument)
T-60	**عزم**	invite
	علك	chew
	غفر	forgive
	غلب	beat, defeat
	غلق	close (door)
	غمز	wink
	فرك	rub, polish
	فرم	chop up, mince
	فلت	escape, get away
T-72	**قتل**	kill; fight
	قسم	divide
T-75	**قعد**	sit; stay; be doing; be off work
	كبس	staple
T-77	**كتب**	write
	كسر	break *(tr.)*
	لمس	touch
	مرق	pass (by); stop by
T-82	**مسك**	hold
	ملك	own
	نتج	produce
	نزف	bleed
	نشر	publish; saw (wood)
	نطق	pronounce
	نقل	move (houses); copy; cheat (in class)
	هبط	land
	هجم	attack
	هلك	become exhausted

Is3 *sound measure* / ③

T-5	**أمر**	instruct; give an order, command
	بسط	display; spread out
	حصد	harvest
	حفر	dig
	حقد	resent
	خبط	crash
	خطف	kidnap, abduct
	خلط	mix
T-35	**ربط**	bind, tie, link, fasten
	رفض	refuse
	شطب	cross out
	صدر	issue
T-56	**طبخ**	cook; prepare (food)

	ظبط	fit *(tr.)*; control; work out (successfully)
	عبط	hug
	عرض	offer, present
	عطس	sneeze
	غطس	dive, submerge
	غمد	(eyes) close *(intr.)*
	فرض	impose (on على); assume, suppose
	فرق	turn *(intr.)*, make a turn
	فصل	separate
	قبض	arrest على
	قرض	suggest, propose
	قصد	mean
	قطش	cut; interrupt
	لبط	kick
T-88	**نطر**	wait
	هجر	abandon, desert
	هرب	escape
	وصف	describe

1s4 *sound measure* / ④

T-93	**وَعد**	promise
	وَعظ	preach

1s5 *sound measure* / ⑤

	بِخِل	become stingy
	تِعِب	get tired
	حِبِل	get pregnant
	حِزِر	guess
	حِزِن	mourn
T-24	**حِضِر**	watch; attend
	حِفِظ	save (file); memorize
	حِلِم	dream
	خِرِس	be quiet, keep silent
	خِسِر	lose (game, money)
T-28	**خِلِص**	stop, finish, end
	خِلِق	be born
	رِبِح	win; gain
T-37	**رِجِع**	return *(intr.)*; come back, go back
	رِضِع	be breastfed, suckle
T-38	**رِكِب**	ride
	زِعِل	get angry/upset
	زِهِق	get bored
	سِكِر	get drunk
T-47	**سِمِع**	hear; listen (to)
	سِهِر	stay up late
	شِبِع	become full (of food)
	شِبِه	resemble; look like
T-51	**شِرِب**	drink; smoke
	شِفِق	pity على
T-54	**ضِحِك**	laugh; lie to, deceive على
	ضِعِف	lose weight
	طِخِن	get fat
T-58	**طِلِع**	go up; ascend; board
	عِرِق	sweat
	عِشِق	love passionately
	عِطِش	become thirsty
	غِرِق	sink
	فِهِم	understand

T-69	**قِبِل**	accept, agree
T-73	**قِدِر**	be able to, can
	قِطِع	cross, pass
	قِلِق	worry, be anxious
	كِرِه	hate
	لِحِق	follow, chase
T-81	**لِعِب**	play
	نِدِم	regret
	نِزِل	go down; descend
	نِشِف	dry *(intr.)*
	نِصِح	put on weight; get fat
	هِلِك	get tired (exhausted)

1s6 *sound measure* / ⑥

	بِعِد	become far
	حِمِل	carry
T-80	**لِبِس**	wear

1s7 *sound measure* / ⑦

T-59	**عِرِف**	know
T-62	**عِمِل**	do, make

1s8 *sound measure* / ⑧

	وِثِق	trust
	وِجِع	hurt *(intr.)*
T-94	**وِقِع**	fall
T-95	**وِقِف**	stand
T-97	**وِلِد**	be born

1s9 *sound measure* / ⑨

T-92	**وُصِل**	arrive

1h1 *hollow measure* / ①

	باض	lay (an egg)
T-6	**باع**	sell
T-18	**جاب**	bring; get
	دان	convict, condemn
	زاح	move (st.) out of the way
	زاد	increase *(intr.)*; add *(tr.)*
	زان	weigh
	شال	remove; take away; pick up, carry
	صاب	hit (a target); afflict
T-53	**صار**	become; happen; start to
	ضاع	get lost
	ضاف	add
	طار	fly
	عاد	repeat
	فاد	be useful
T-65	**فاق**	get up; wake up
	قاس	measure
	ناك	fuck

1h2 *hollow measure* / ②

	باس	kiss
	تاب	repent
	ثار	erupt
	جاع	become hungry
	حاز	obtain, get على

	خان	betray
	داب	melt *(intr.)*, dissolve *(intr.)*, thaw *(intr.)*
	دار	turn (tr/intr.); roam around
	داق	taste
T-34	**راح**	go
	راق	calm down
T-40	**زار**	visit
	ساق	drive
	شاط	shoot (goal); kick (ball); burn (food)
T-48	**شاف**	see; look (at)
	صام	fast
	طاف	float; flood
	عار	lend
	عاز	need; require
	عاش	live
	غاص	dive, submerge
	فات	enter; pass (by)
	فاز	win (game)
	فاش	float
	فاق	remember
	قاد	lead
T-70	**قال**	say; tell (to لـ)
	قام	rise; get up
	كان	be, am, is, are, was, were
	لام	blame
	مات	die

1h2 *hollow measure* / ③

	خاف	be afraid of, fear مِن
	طال	reach
T-84	**نام**	sleep

1d1 *defective measure* / ①

	برى	sharpen a pencil
	بنى	build
	جرى	(water) run
	جلى	wash (dishes)
	حبى	crawl
	حشى	stuff, fill
	دعا	pray
	رشى	bribe
T-39	**رمى**	throw
	سقى	water (a plant)
	شكى	complain
	صقى	irrigate
	طوى	fold
	غلى	boil (tr; liquid) (vs سلق)
	قلى	fry *(tr.)*
	كوى	iron
	لغى	cancel
	محى	erase
	مضى	sign
	نهى	end, finish
	نَوى	intend
	هدى	give as a gift

1d2 *defective measure* / ②

	رعى	graze
	عمى	go blind

T-74 قرا read

1d3 *defective measure* / ③

T-8 **بِقي** become; stay; remain
رِضي be pleased
غِفي fall asleep
غِلي become expensive
فِضي become empty
T-86 **نِسي** forget
وِعي wake up *(intr.)*

1d4 *defective measure* / ④

بِكي cry
T-26 **حِكي** talk; speak; tell (a story)
حِمى protect
T-83 **مِشي** walk, go

1d irr. *irregular defective measure* /

T-61 **عطى** give

1g1 *geminate measure* / ①

بخّ spray
بلّ wet, dampen
جرّ drag, pull
جزّ shear (a sheep)
T-20 **حبّ** like, love, want
T-23 **حسّ** feel; sense
حفّ rub
حكّ scratch, itch, scrape
حلّ solve
دقّ knock; beat, palpitate; hammer; ring
دلّ indicate, point to على; show the way; guide
ردّ reply; answer على; return; bring back
رفّ blink
رنّ ring
زتّ throw; throw away
سبّ curse, swear
سدّ block, seal
شدّ pull; tighten; drag; attract
شكّ doubt
شمّ smell *(tr.)*
عدّ count
غشّ cheat
فزّ jump
فكّ undo, untie, unbutton, remove
فلّ leave; depart
قلّ decrease, reduce *(intr.)*
كبّ spill
لحّ pressure; insist
لفّ turn; wrap
لمّ gather, collect
مدّ extend; stretch *(tr.)*
نفّ blow one's nose
نقّ complain; nag
هبّ blow
هدّ demolish, break down
هزّ shake

	همّ	worry, trouble *(tr.)*

1g2 *geminate measure I ②*

T-25	**حطّ**	put, place; lay; deposit (in bank)
	خصّ	belong; concern
	خضّ	shake; shock
	شخّ	urinate, pee, piss
	صبّ	pour
	صحّ	recover, get better; heal, cure; be correct
	صفّ	park (car); sort (in rows)
	ضبّ	tidy up, put away; gather, collect; pack (a suitcase)
	ضمّ	embrace; bring together
	طبّ	doze off
	طجّ	(ball) bounce
	قحّ	cough
	قصّ	cut
	مرّ	pass (by); stop by
	نطّ	jump

1g3 *geminate measure I ③*

T-55	**ضلّ**	remain (in a place), stay; keep doing
	عضّ	bite

1 irr. *irregular measure I*

T-1	**إجا**	come
T-2	**أخد**	take
T-4	**أكل**	eat

2s *sound measure II*

	أثّر	affect; influence
	أجّر	rent (لـ to)
	أجّل	postpone
	أخّر	delay *(tr.)*
	أدّب	discipline
	أدّن	call to prayer
	أسّس	found, establish
	أكّد	confirm, check, verify, assure
	ألّف	compose
	أهّل	train, qualify, welcome
	بدّل	replace
	بشّر	preach (about بِـ)
	بطّل	quit
	بكّل	button, fasten, buckle
T-9	**بلّش**	begin, start
	بلّغ	report, inform
	بوّل	urinate, pee
	بيّض	whiten
	بيّن	demonstrate, show, reveal
	ثبّت	fix (in place), fasten, establish
	جدّد	renew
	جرّب	try (out)
	جمّع	gather, collect
	جنّد	recruit, enlist
	جهّز	prepare
	حدّد	set, fix, define

حرّر liberate

T-22 **حرّك** move *(tr.)*

حرّم forbid (in religion)

حسّن improve *(tr.)*, make better

حضّر prepare

حقّق realize, achieve; verify, check

خبّر tell, inform

خرّب vandalize

خرّط chop (up)

خزّق tear

خطّط plan

خفّف lessen, lighten, slow down *(tr.)*

T-29 **خلّص** finish, terminate

خلّص finish, end, complete, accomplish

خوّف frighten, scare

خيّط sew

دخّن smoke

درّب train

درّس teach

دلّك massage

دمّر dammage

دوّب melt *(tr.)*, dissolve *(tr.)*, thaw *(tr.)*

دوّر look for, search (for على)

ديّن lend (money)

ذكّر remind

رتّب arrange

رجّع give back, return *(tr.)*

رشّح nominate

رضّع breastfeed

رقّع patch, darn

ركّب pick up, give a ride to

زبّط adjust; trim (beard)

زعّل anger, upset

زقّف applaud

زهّق bore (make feel bored)

سبّب cause

سجّل record

سخّن heat up

سدّد settle, pay off (debt)

T-45 **سكّر** close *(tr.)*, shut *(tr.)*

سلّم deliver; greet على

سوّد blacken

سيّج fence in

شجّع cheer, encourage

شخّر snore

شخّص diagnose

شغّل operate, make work; hire, employ

شكّل form

شلّح undress *(tr.)*

صحّح correct

صدّق believe

صرّح state, declare

صرّف change money; break a bill, make change; inflect, conjugate, decline

صلّح repair, fix; edit, correct

	صمّد	save, put aside (money)
	صمّم	design
	صوّت	vote
	صوّر	photograph; photocopy
	ضحّك	make laugh
	ضرّط	fart
	ضيّع	lose
	طرّز	embroider
	طلّع	take out; take up(stairs)
	طلّق	divorce
	عبّر	express عن
	عجّز	age, grow old
	عذّب	torture
	عرّف	introduce (someone to على)
	عصّب	become angry; bandage
	عفّن	rot, decay *(intr.)*
	علّق	hang *(tr.)*
	علّم	teach
	عمّد	baptize
	عمّر	build
	عيّط	yell, shout, scream
	عيّن	appoint
T-63	**غسّل**	wash
	غمّد	close (eyes)
T-64	**غيّر**	change *(tr.)*
	فسّر	explain
	فضّل	prefer
T-68	**فكّر**	think (about في)
	فوّت	let in, admit; put in
	فوّق	remind
	فيّق	wake *(tr.)*
	قارن	compare
	قدّر	appreciate; estimate, value
	قدّم	present, offer; submit; apply (to على)
	قرّر	decide
	قطّع	cut
	قفّل	lock
	قلّل	reduce, decrease *(tr.)*
	كبّر	enlarge
	كتّر	increase *(tr.)*
T-78	**كذّب**	lie
	كشّر	frown
	كلّف	cost *(intr.)*
	كمّل	continue
	كنّس	sweep
	كوّن	create, form
	لحّق	manage (to do); catch up with
	لحّن	tune (instrument)
	لزّق	stick, cling
	لوّن	color
	مثّل	act, perform; represent
	مشّط	comb
	موّل	finance
	ميّز	distinguish
	نبّه	warn
	نزّل	download; make lower; drop off
	نشّف	dry *(tr.)*

نضّف clean

نظّم organize

نقّد carry out, perform

نمّل be numb, tingle

هرّب smuggle

وجّع hurt *(tr.)*

ودّع bid farewell

وسّع widen

وصّل deliver

وظّف employ

وفّر provide; supply

وقّع drop; sign

وقّف stop *(tr.)*

T-96 **وَقّف** stop (tr./intr.)

ولّد give birth

ولّع light (cigarette)

2d *defective measure II*

أدّى perform, carry out

خبّى hide

T-30 **خلّى** make, cause; allow, let; keep

رخّى relax

سلّى entertain

سمّى name, call

شتّى rain

صلّى pray (ritual prayer)

ضوّى turn on, switch on

طفّى extinguish; turn off, switch off

عبّى fill; fill in (form), fill out (form)

علّى turn up (volume); make high

عوّى bark

غطّى cover

غنّى sing

فضّى empty, vacate; unpack *(tr.)*

مضّى spend (time)

نقّى pick, choose, select

وعّى wake (up), rouse

3s *sound measure III*

آمن believe (in بِـ)

بادر initiate

بادل reciprocate

بارك bless

جادل argue (about على)

جاوب answer, reply, respond to

حافظ maintain على

T-19 **حاوَل** try; attempt

خانق fight with; argue with

دافع defend

راجع check, revise, review

رافق accompany

راهن bet

T-41 **ساعد** help, assist

سافر travel

سامح forgive

ساوم haggle over, bargain

ضايق annoy, bother, disturb

عاكس oppose

عالج cure, treat

فاجئ surprise

قابل interview

لاحظ notice

لاحق chase, pursue

مارس practice, exercise

ناقش discuss

هاجم assault, attack

واجه face

وافق approve of

3d *defective measure III*

جازى punish

حاكى talk

ساوى equal; do

عانى suffer

T-79 **لاقى** find

نادى call

4s *defective measure IV*

أصْدر publish

T-3 **أعْلن** announce, declare

أنْكر deny

5s *sound measure V*

تْأجّل be delayed

تْأخّر be late

تْأدّب behave

تْأسّف be sorry, regret

تْجمّد freeze *(intr.)*

تْجنّب avoid

تْجوّز get married (to)

تْحجّب wear a hijab

تْحرّك move *(intr.)*

تْحسّن improve *(intr.)*, get better

تْحمّل bear, endure, tolerate

تْحمّم take a bath

تْحوّل change, turn into

تْخرّج graduate (from مِن)

تْخصّص major (in بـِ), specialize (in بـِ)

تْخلّص get rid of مِن

تْخيّل imagine

تْدرّب practice على

تْديّن borrow (money); become religious

تْذكّر remember

تْردّد hesitate

تْروّق have breakfast

تْزلّج ski

تْسجّل enroll

تْسكّر close *(intr.)*

تْشرْدق choke (on بـِ food/object), swallow the wrong way

تْصرّف behave

تْصطّح nap

تْصوّر be photographed; imagine

تْطلّع look at في/بـِ

تْطلّق get divorced

تْطوّر develop *(intr.)*

تْعرّف meet, be acquainted with

T-12 **تْعلّم** learn, study

تْعوّد get used to, become accustomed to

تْغيرّ change *(intr.)*

تْفرّج watch على

تْفوّع vomit, throw up

تْقطّب get stitches

تْكوّن be composed of

تْمرّن practice (sport); exercise, work out

تْنفّس breathe

تْوجّه head toward لـ

تْوظّف obtain employment

تْوقّع expect

5d *defective measure V*

تْبنّى adopt

تْخطّى speed, go over the speed limit

تْدشّى burp, belch

تْرجّى beg, plead

تْرقّى get promoted (at work)

تْسلّى have fun, enjoy oneself

تْسمّى be named, be called

تْعشّى have dinner

T-13 **تْغدّى** have lunch

تْمشّى go for a walk

T-17 **تْمنّى** hope; wish

تْوضّى perform ritual ablutions

تْوفّى pass away

6s *sound measure VI*

تّاوب yawn

تْجاوز pass, overtake

تْخانق argue, fight, quarrel *(intr.)*

تْشاءم be pessimistic

تْظاهر demonstrate, protest

T-11 **تْعامل** treat مع; deal with مع, work with مع

تْفاءل be optimistic

تْفاجئ be surprised

تْفاهم understand each other

تْقاعد retire

6d *defective measure VI*

T-14 **تْفادى** avoid, dodge

7s *sound measure VII*

T-85 **نْبسط** have fun, enjoy oneself

نْتزع go bad, spoil *(intr.)*, become ruined

نْحرق burn *(intr.)*; become burned

نْشغل become busy

نْطرد get fired

نْفجر explode *(intr.)*; erupt

نْقبض get arrested

نْكسر break *(intr.)*

7h *hollow measure VII*

T-89 **نْقال** be said

نْهار collapse

7d defective measure VII

T-90 **نْلغى** be canceled

7g geminate measure VII

T-87 **نْضمّ** join

8s sound measure VIII

بْتسم smile

تّصل contact مع/بِ; connect مع/بِ

تّفق agree (with مع); get along with مع

جْتمع meet (with مع)

حْتاج need

حْترم respect

T-21 **حْتفل** celebrate

خْتلف disagree with مع; differ مع/مِن

خْتنق choke, suffocate

رْتكِب commit (a crime)

سْتلم receive

شْترك join, participate in بِـ

T-50 **شْتغل** work (as)

عْتبر consider

عْتذر apologize (to لـ/ forعلى)

عْترف admit to, confess

عْتقد think (believe)

عْتقل arrest

عْتمد depend on على

غْتصب rape

فْترض suppose

فْتكر think (I think...)

قْترح suggest

كْتشف discover

لْتزم comply with, observe

نْتخب elect

نْتظر wait

نْتقد criticize

8h hollow measure VIII

خْتار choose

T-36 **رْتاح** rest, relax

سْتعار borrow (something)

شْتاق miss; long for

صْطاد fish, hunt

8d defective measure VIII

حْتوى contain

خْتفى disappear

دّعى claim

T-49 **شْترى** buy

عْتدى assault, attack على

لْتقى meet up with بِـ

نْتهى end *(intr.)*

8g geminate measure VIII

حْتجّ protest

حْتلّ occupy

T-91 **هْتمّ** be interested (in بِـ), care (about بِـ)

9s sound measure IX

	بْيضّ	become white, become pale
T-27	**حْمرّ**	turn red; blush
	خْضرّ	turn green
	زْرقّ	turn blue; bruise
	سْمرّ	tan
	سْودّ	become black/dark
	صْفرّ	turn yellow

10s sound measure X

	سْتأجر	rent (from)
	سْتجْوب	interrogate
	سْتخْدم	use
T-43	**سْتعْمل**	use
	سْتغْرب	consider strange
	سْتقْبل	welcome, greet
	سْتكشف	explore
	سْتمْتع	enjoy

10h hollow measure X

	سْتشار	consult
	سْتقال	resign

10d defective measure X

	سْتغنى	do without, live without
	سْتنّى	wait

10g geminate measure X

	سْتعدّ	get ready

10 irr. irregular measure X

-	سْتاهل	deserve
T-44	**سْتهنّى**	enjoy بِـ

11s sound measure XI

	بحْلق	stare, gaze
	بخْشش	tip (give a gratuity)
	بخْوش	puncture
	برْطل	bribe
	برْهن	prove
	بصْبص	peep
	تْرجم	translate
T-16	**تلْفن**	telephone, phone, call
	ختْير	age; get old
	دوْبل	pass, overtake
	سَيْطر	control
	فرْكش	trip *(tr.)*
	كزْدر	hang out (with friends)
	لخْبط	confuse; mix up
	نرْفز	get annoyed
	هرْول	jog, go jogging
	وَشْوش	whisper

11d defective measure XI

T-67	**فرْجى**	show (to على)
	فرْشى	brush

12s sound measure XI

	تْترْجم	be translated

تفْركش trip *(intr.)*

T-15 **تْلخْبط** be confused; get mixed up; err, make a mistake

F *foreign borrowings*

داوْنْلود، يْداوْنْلِد download

سايْف، يْسايِف save

Arabic – English Index

أثّر affect; influence 2s

إجا come *(irr.)* **T-1**

أجّر rent (لـ to) 2s

أجّل postpone 2s

أخد take *(irr.)* **T-2**

أخّر delay *(tr.)* 2s

أدّب discipline 2s

أدّن call to prayer 2s

أدّى perform, carry out يْوَدّي 2d

أسّس found, establish 2s

أصْدر publish 4s

أعْلن announce, declare 4s **T-3**

أكّد confirm, check, verify, assure 2s

أكل eat *(irr.)* **T-4**

ألّف compose 2s

أمر instruct; give an order, command 1s3 **T-5**

آمن believe (in بـِ) 3s

أنْكر deny 4s

أهّل train, qualify, welcome 2s

باد initiate 3s

باد reciprocate 3s

بار bless 3s

با kiss 1h2

با lay (an egg) 1h1

ب sell 1h1 **T-6**

بْتس smile 8s

بح dig 1s1

بحْلق stare, gaze 11s

بخّ spray 1g1

بخْشش tip (give a gratuity) 11s

بخع humiliate (cause to lose face) 1s1

بخِل become stingy 1s5

بخْوش puncture 11s

بدّل replace 2s

برد file (down) 1s2

برد get cold 1s2

برز become clear 1s2

برش grate 1s2

برش grate 1s2

برْطل bribe 11s

برم turn (around); visit, roam 1s2 **T-7**

برْهن prove 11s

برى sharpen a pencil 1d1

بزق spit 1s2

بسط display; spread out 1s3

بشّر preach (about بـِ) 2s

بصْبص peep 11s

بطّل quit 2s

بعت send; mail 1s1

بِعِد become far 1s6

بِقي become; stay; remain 1d3 **T-8**

بكّل button, fasten, buckle 2s

بِكي cry 1d4

بلّ wet, dampen 1g1

بلّش begin, start 2s **T-9**

بلع swallow 1s1
بلّغ report, inform 2s
بنى build 1d1
بوّل urinate, pee 2s
بْيض become white, become pale 9s
بيّض whiten 2s
بيّن demonstrate, show, reveal 2s
تاب repent 1h2
تْأجّل be delayed 5s
تْأخّر be late 5s
تْأدّب behave 5s
تْأسّف be sorry, regret 5s
تّاوب yawn 6s
تبع follow (a recipe, etc.) 1s1
تْبنّى adopt 5d
تْترْجم be translated 12s
تْجاوز pass, overtake 6s
تْجمّد freeze *(intr.)* 5s
تْجنّب avoid 5s
تْجوّز get married (to) 5s
تْحجّب wear a hijab 5s
تْحرّك move *(intr.)* 5s
تْحسّن improve *(intr.)*, get better 5s
تْحمّل bear, endure, tolerate 5s
تْحمّم take a bath 5s
تْحوّل change, turn into 5s
تْخانق argue, fight, quarrel *(intr.)* 6s
تْخرّج graduate (from مِن) 5s
تْخصّص major (in بِـ), specialize (in بِـ) 5s
تْخطّى speed, go over the speed limit 5d
تْخلّص get rid of مِن 5s
تْخيّل imagine 5s
تْدرّب practice على 5s
تْدشّى burp, belch 5d
تْديّن borrow (money); become religious 5s
تْذكّر remember 5s
ترْجم translate 11s
تْرجّى beg, plead 5d
تْردّد hesitate 5s
تْرقّى get promoted (at work) 5d
ترك leave; quit 1s2 **T-10**
تْروّق have breakfast 5s
تْزلّج ski 5s
تْسجّل enroll 5s
تْسكّر close *(intr.)* 5s
تْسلّى have fun, enjoy oneself 5d
تْسمّى be named, be called 5d
تْشاءم be pessimistic 6s
تْشرْدق choke (on بِـ food/object), swallow the wrong way 5s
تْصرّف behave 5s
تْصطّح nap 5s
تّصل contact مع/بِـ; connect مع/بِـ 8s
تْصوّر have one's picture taken, be photographed; imagine 5s
تْطلّع look at في/بِـ 5s
تْطلّق get divorced 5s
تْطوّر develop *(intr.)* 5s
تْظاهر demonstrate, protest 6s
تْعامل treat مع; deal with مع, work with مع 6s **T-11**
تِعِب get tired 1s5
تْعرّف meet, be acquainted with 5s
تْعشّى have dinner 5d
تْعلّم learn, study 5s **T-12**
تْعوّد get used to, become accustomed to 5s
تْغدّى have lunch 5d **T-13**
تْغيّر change *(intr.)* 5s
تْفاءل be optimistic 6s
تْفاجئ be surprised 6s
تْفادى avoid, dodge 6d **T-14**
تْفاهم understand each other 6s
تْفرّج watch على5s
تْفرْكش trip *(intr.)* 12s
تّفق agree (with مع); get along with مع8
تْفوّع vomit, throw up 5s

تْقاعد retire 6s

تْقطّب get stitches 5s

تْكوّن be composed of 5s

تْلخْبط be confused; get mixed up; err, make a mistake 12s **T-15**

تلْفن telephone, phone, call 11s **T-16**

تْمرّن practice (sport); exercise, work out 5s

تْمشّى go for a walk 5d

تْمنّى hope; wish 5d **T-17**

تْنفّس breathe 5s

تهم accuse 1s2

تْوجّه head toward لـ 5s

تْوضّى perform ritual ablutions 5d

تْوظّف obtain employment 5s

تْوفّى pass away 5d

تْوقّع expect 5s

ثار erupt 1h2

ثبّت fix (in place), fasten, establish 2s

جاب bring; get 1h1 **T-18**

جادل argue (about على) 3s

جازى punish 3d

جاع become hungry 1h2

جاوب answer, reply, respond to 3s

جبر force (someone to do) 1s2

جْتمع meet (with مع) 8s

جدّد renew 2s

جذب attract 1s2

ج drag, pull 1g1

جرّب try (out) 2s

جرح wound, injure, hurt 1s1

جرى (water) run 1d1

ج shear (a sheep) 1g1

جلق scratch 1s2

جلى wash (dishes) 1d1

جمع add, add up; harvest 1s1

جمّع gather, collect 2s

ج recruit, enlist 2s

ج prepare 2s

حاز على obtain, get 1h2

حافظ maintain على 3s

حاكى talk 3d

حاوَل try; attempt 3s **T-19**

حبّ like, love, want 1g1 **T-20**

حبس imprison 1s2

حِبِل get pregnant 1s5

حبى crawl 1d1

حْتاج need 8s

حْتجّ protest 8g

حْترم respect 8s

حْتفل celebrate 8s **T-21**

حْتلّ occupy 8g

حْتوى contain 8d

حجز book, reserve 1s2

حدّد set, fix, define 2s

حرث plow 1s2

حرّر liberate 2s

حرس guard 1s2

حرق burn 1s2

حرّك move *(tr.)* 2s

حرّك move *(tr.)* 2s **T-22**

حرم deprive 1s2

حرّم forbid (in religion) 2s

حِزِر guess 1s5

حِزِن mourn 1s5

حسّ feel; sense 1g1 **T-23**

حسب calculate 1s2

حسّن improve *(tr.)*, make better 2s

حشى stuff, fill 1d1

حصد harvest 1s3

حصل obtain على 1s1

حضّر prepare 2s

حِضِر watch; attend 1s5 **T-24**

حطّ put, place; lay; deposit (in bank) 1g3 **T-25**

حفّ rub 1g1

حفر dig 1s3

حِفِظ save (file); memorize 1s5

حقد resent 1s3
حقّق realize, achieve; verify, check 2s
حكّ scratch, itch, scrape 1g1
حكم govern 1s2
حِكي talk; speak; tell (a story) 1d4 **T-26**
حلّ solve 1g1
حلب milk 1s2
حلف swear (by?) 1s2
حلق shave 1s2
حِلِم dream 1s5
حْمرّ turn red; blush 9s **T-27**
حِمِل carry 1s6
حِمي protect 1d4
خاف be afraid of, fear مِن 1h3
خان betray 1h2
خانق fight with; argue with 3s
خبّر tell, inform 2s
خبز bake 1s2
خبط crash 1s3
خبّى hide 2d
خْتار choose 8h
خْتفى disappear 8d
خْتلف disagree with مع; differ مع/مِن 8s
ختم conclude, finish; stamp 1s2
خْتنق choke, suffocate 8s
ختْير age; get old 11s
خدع deceive 1s1
خدم serve 1s2
خرّب vandalize 2s
خِرِس be quiet, keep silent 1s5
خرّط chop (up) 2s
خزّق tear 2s
خِسِر lose (game, money) 1s5
خصّ belong; concern 1g2
خضّ shake; shock 1g2
خْضرّ turn green 9s
خطّط plan 2s
خطف kidnap, abduct 1s3
خفّف lessen, lighten, slow down *(tr.)* 2s
خلّص finish, end, complete, accomplish 2s
خلّص finish, terminate 2s **T-29**
خِلِص stop, finish, end 1s5 **T-28**
خلط mix 1s3
خلع snatch 1s1
خِلِق be born 1s5
خلق create 1s2
خلّى make, cause; allow, let; keep 2d **T-30**
خوّف frighten, scare 2s
خيّط sew 2s
داب melt *(intr.)*, dissolve *(intr.)*, thaw *(intr.)* 1h2
دار turn (tr/intr.); roam around 1h2
دافع defend 3s
داق taste 1h2
دان convict, condemn 1h1
داوْنْلود (يْداوْنْلِد) download *(irr.)* (foreign)
دخّن smoke 2s
درّب train 2s
درس study 1s2 **T-31**
درّس teach 2s
دعا pray 1d1
دعس step 1s1
دعس tread on على1s1
دّعى claim 8d *(irr.)*
because dd
دفش push, shove 1s2
دفع pay 1s1 **T-32**
دفن bury 1s2
دقّ knock; beat, palpitate; hammer; ring 1g1
دقر touch 1s1 **T-33**
دلّ indicate, point to على; show the way; guide 1g1
دلق pour 1s2
دلّك massage 2s
دمّر dammage 2s

ده paint 1s1
دوّ melt *(tr.)*, dissolve *(tr.)*, thaw *(tr.)* 2s
دوْ pass, overtake 11s
د look for, search (for على) 2s
د lend (money) 2s
ذ mention 1s2
ذ remind 2s
راج check, revise, review 3s
ر go 1h2 **T-34**
راف accompany 3s
ر calm down 1h2
راه bet 3s
ر win; gain 1s5
ر bind, tie, link, fasten 1s3 **T-35**
رْ rest, relax 8h **T-36**
رتّ arrange 2s
رْتك commit (a crime, etc) 8s
ر give back, return *(tr.)* 2s
رج return *(intr.)*; come back, go back 1s5 **T-37**
رخ relax 2d
reply; answer على; return; bring back 1g1
ر (God) bless 1s2
رس draw 1s2
رشّ nominate 2s
رش bribe 1d1
رض be breastfed, suckle 1s5
رضّ breastfeed 2s
رض be pleased 1d3
ر graze 1d2
ر blink 1g1
رفض refuse 1s3
ر raise 1s1
رقص dance 1s2
ر patch, darn 2s
ركّ pick up, give a ride to 2s
رك ride 1s5 **T-38**

ركض run 1s2
رمز represent, symbolize 1s2
رمى throw 1d1 **T-39**
رنّ ring 1g1
زاح move (st.) out of the way 1h1
زاد increase *(intr.)*; add *(tr.)* 1h1
زار visit 1h2 **T-40**
زان weigh 1h1
زبّط adjust; trim (beard) 2s
زتّ throw; throw away 1g1
زحط slip 1s1
زرع plant (a seed), grow (a plant) 1s1
زْرقّ turn blue; bruise *(intr.)* 9s
زعب kick; speak harshly 1s1
زعّل anger, upset 2s
زِعِل get angry/upset 1s5
زقّف applaud 2s
زهّق bore (make feel bored) 2s
زِهِق get bored 1s5
ساعد help, assist 3s **T-41**
سافر travel 3s
ساق drive 1h2
سأل ask 1s1 **T-42**
سامح forgive 3s
ساوم haggle over, bargain 3s
ساوى equal; do 3d
سايْف، يْسايِف save *(irr.)* (foreign)
سبّ curse, swear 1g1
سبّب cause 2s
سبح swim 1s1
سْتأجر rent (from) 10s
سْتاهل deserve 10 *(irr.)*
سْتجْوب interrogate 10s
سْتخْدم use 10s
سْتشار consult 10h
سْتعار borrow (something) 8h
سْتعدّ get ready 10g
سْتعْمل use 10s **T-43**
سْتغْرب consider strange 10s

سْتغنى do without, live without 10d
سْتقال resign 10h
سْتقْبل welcome, greet 10s
سْتكشف explore 10s
سْتلم receive 8s
سْتمْتع enjoy 10s
سْتنّى wait 10d
سْتهنّى enjoy بِـ 10 *(irr.)* **T-44**
سجّل record 2s
سحب withdraw 1s1
سخّن heat up 2s
سدّ block, seal 1g1
سدّد settle, pay off (debt) 2s
سرق steal 1s2
سعل cough 1s2
سفق hit, strike; slam 1s2
سقط fail 1s2
سقى water (a plant) 1d1
سكت be quiet, shut up 1s2
سكّر close *(tr.)*, shut *(tr.)* 2s **T-45**
سِكِر get drunk 1s5
سكن live 1s2 **T-46**
سلق boil (food) 1s2
سلّم deliver; greet على 2s
سلّى entertain 2d
سمح allow, permit 1s1
سْمرّ tan 9s
سمع hear; listen (to) 1s5 **T-47**
سمّى name, call 2d
سند support 1s2
سِهِر stay up late 1s5
سْودّ become black, get dark 9s
سوّد blacken 2s
سيّج fence in 2s
سَيْطر control 11s
شاط shoot (goal); kick (ball); burn (food) 1h2
شاف see; look (at) 1h2 **T-48**
شال remove; take away; pick up, carry 1h1
شِبِع become full (of food) 1s5
شِبِه resemble; look like 1s5
شْتاق miss; long for 8h
شْترك join, participate in بِـ 8s
شْترى buy 8d **T-49**
شْتغل work (as) 8s **T-50**
شتّى rain 2d
شجّع cheer, encourage 2s
شحد beg (for money) 1s1
شخّ urinate, pee, piss 1g2
شخّر snore 2s
شخّص diagnose 2s
شدّ pull; tighten; drag; attract 1g1
شرب drink; smoke 1s5 **T-51**
شرح explain 1s1
شرق (sun) rise 1s2
شطب cross out 1s3
شطف rinse 1s2
شعر feel بِـ 1s2
شغّل operate, make work; hire, employ 2s
شِفِق pity على 1s5
شقل lift and carry 1s2
شكّ doubt 1g1
شكر thank 1s2 **T-52**
شكّل form 2s
شكى complain 1d1
شلّح undress *(tr.)* 2s
شلح undress, take off (clothes), remove (clothes) 1s1
شمّ smell *(tr.)* 1g1
شمل include 1s2
صاب hit (a target); afflict 1h1
صار become; happen; start to 1h1 **T-53**
صام fast 1h2
صبّ pour 1g2
صبغ dye one's hair 1s2

صح recover, get better; heal, cure; be correct 1g2

صحّ correct 2s

صد issue 1s3

صدّق believe 2s

صرّ state, declare 2s

صرّف change money; break a bill, make change; inflect (word), conjugate (verb), decline (word) 2s

صرف spend (money); change (money); fire, dismiss (from a job) 1s2

صْط fish, hunt 8h

ص park (car); sort (in rows) 1g2

صْ turn yellow 9s

صن irrigate 1d1

ص repair, fix; edit, correct 2s

ص pray (ritual prayer) 2d

ص save, put aside (money) 2s

ص design 2s

ص manufacture 1s1

ص vote 2s

ص photograph; photocopy 2s

ض get lost 1h1

ض add 1h1

ض annoy, bother, disturb 3s

ض tidy up, put away; gather, collect; pack (a suitcase) 1g2

ض laugh; lie to, deceive على 1s5 **T-54**

ض make laugh 2s

ض hit, beat; multiply 1s2

ض fart 2s

ض lose weight 1s5

remain (in a place), stay; keep doing g3 **T-55**

embrace?; bring together? 1g2

leave; go out 1s1

turn on, switch on 2d

lose 2s

fly 1h1

طاف float; flood 1h2

طال reach 1h3

طبّ doze off 1g2

طبخ cook; prepare (food) 1s3 **T-56**

طبع print 1s1

طجّ (ball) bounce 1g2

طحن grind 1s1

طِخِن get fat 1s5

طرح subtract 1s1

طرد fire 1s2

طرّز embroider 2s

طفّى extinguish; turn off, switch off 2d

طلب request, order 1s2 **T-57**

طِلِع go up; ascend; board (flight, etc) 1s5 **T-58**

طلّع take out; take up(stairs) 2s

طلّق divorce 2s

طوى fold 1d1

ظبط fit *(tr.)*; control; work out (successfully) 1s3

ظهر appear 1s1

عاد repeat 1h1

عار lend 1h2

عاز need; require 1h2

عاش live 1h2

عاكس oppose 3s

عالج cure, treat 3s

عانى suffer 3d

عبّر express عن 2s

عبس frown, knit one's brow, scowl 1s2

عبط hug 1s3

عبّى fill; fill in/out (a form) 2d

عْتبر consider 8s

عْتدى assault, attack على8d

عْتذر apologize (to لـ/ forعلى) 8s

عْترف admit to, confess 8s

عْتقد think (believe) 8s

عْتقل arrest 8s

عْتمد depend on على8s

عجب please, appeal to 1s2
عجّز age, grow old 2s
عدّ count 1g1
عذّب torture 2s
عذر excuse 1s2
عرض offer, present 1s3
عرّف introduce (someone to على) 2s
عِرِف know 1s7 **T-59**
عِرِق sweat 1s5
عزف play (instrument) 1s2
عزم invite 1s2 **T-60**
عِشِق love passionately 1s5
عصّب become angry; bandage 2s
عضّ bite 1g3
عطس sneeze 1s3
عِطِش become thirsty 1s5
عطى give 1d *(irr.)* (aa-ai) **T-61**
عفّن rot, decay *(intr.)* 2s
علّق hang *(tr.)* 2s
علك chew 1s2
علّم teach 2s
علّى turn up (volume); make high 2d
عمّد baptize 2s
عمّر build 2s
عِمِل do, make 1s7 **T-62**
عمى go blind 1d2
عوّى bark 2d
عيّط yell, shout, scream 2s
عيّن appoint 2s
غاص dive, submerge 1h2
غْتصب rape 8s
غِرِق sink 1s5
غسّل wash 2s **T-63**
غشّ cheat 1g1
غطس dive, submerge 1s3
غطّى cover 2d
غفر forgive 1s2
غِفِي fall asleep 1d3
غلب beat, defeat 1s2
غلق close (door) 1s2
غلى boil (tr; liquid) 1d1
غِلِي become expensive 1d3
غمد (eyes) close *(intr.)* 1s3
غمّد close (eyes) 2s
غمز wink 1s2
غنّى sing 2d
غيّر change *(tr.)* 2s **T-64**
فات enter; pass (by) 1h2
فاجئ surprise 3s
فاد be useful 1h1
فاز win (game) 1h2
فاش float 1h2
فاق get up; wake up 1h1 **T-65**
فاق remember 1h2
فتح open 1s1 **T-66**
فْترض suppose 8s
فتكر think (I think...) 8s
فحص examine 1s1
فرْجى show (to على) 11d **T-67**
فرْشى brush 11d
فرض impose (on على); assume, suppose 1s3
فرق turn *(intr.)*, make a turn 1s3
فرك rub, polish 1s2
فرْكش trip *(tr.)* 11s
فرم chop up, mince 1s2
فزّ jump 1g1
فسّر explain 2s
فصل separate 1s3
فضّل prefer 2s
فضّى empty, vacate; unpack *(tr.)* 2d
فِضِي become empty 1d3
فقس click on على 1s1
فكّ undo, untie, unbutton, remove 1g1
فكّر think (about في) 2s **T-68**
فلّ leave; depart 1g1
فلت escape, get away 1s2
فلح plow (field); work hard 1s1

فِهِم understand 1s5 **T-69**
فوّت let in, admit; put in 2s
فوّق remind 2s
فيّق wake *(tr.)* 2s
قابل interview 3s
قاد lead 1h2
قارن compare 2s
قاس measure 1h1
قال say; tell (to لـ) 1h2 **T-70**
قام rise; get up 1h2
قبض arrest على 1s3
قبض earn 1s1 **T-71**
قبِل accept, agree 1s5
قْترح suggest 8s
قتل kill; fight 1s2 **T-72**
قحّ cough 1g2
قدّر appreciate; estimate, value 2s
قِدِر be able to, can 1s5 **T-73**
قدّم present, offer; submit; apply (to على) 2s
قرا read 1d2 **T-74**
قرّر decide 2s
قرض suggest, propose 1s3
قسم divide 1s2
قصّ cut 1g2
قصد mean 1s3
قطش cut; interrupt 1s3
قطِ cross, pass 1s5
قطّ cut 2s
قع sit; stay; be doing; be off work 1s2 **T-75**
قفّ lock 2s
ق decrease, reduce *(intr.)* 1g1
قلِ worry, be anxious 1s5
قلّ reduce, decrease *(tr.)* 2s
قل fry *(tr.)* 1d1
ق convince 1s1
ك be, am, is, are, was, were 1h2 **T-76**
ك spill 1g1

كبّر enlarge 2s
كبر grow (up); get big 1s1
كبس staple 1s2
كتب write 1s2 **T-77**
كترّ increase *(tr.)* 2s
كْتشف discover 8s
كذّب lie 2s **T-78**
كرِه hate 1s5
كزْدر hang out (with friends) 11s
كسب win, gain, acquire 1s1
كسر break *(tr.)* 1s2
كشّر frown 2s
كلّف cost *(intr.)* 2s
كمّل continue 2s
كنّس sweep 2s
كوّن create, form 2s
كوى iron 1d1
لاحظ notice 3s
لاحق chase, pursue 3s
لاقى find 3d **T-79**
لام blame 1h2
لِبِس wear 1s6 **T-80**
لبط kick 1s3
لْتزم comply with, observe 8s
لْتقى meet up with بـِ 8d
لحّ pressure; insist ? 1g1
لحس lick 1s1
لِحِق follow, chase 1s5
لحّق manage (to do); catch up with (someone) 2s
لحّن tune (instrument) 2s
لخْبط confuse; mix up 11s
لزّق stick, cling 2s
لِعِب play 1s5 **T-81**
لغى cancel 1d1
لفّ turn; wrap 1g1
لقط catch 1s1
لمّ gather, collect 1g1
لمس touch 1s2

لمع shine 1s1
لوّن color 2s
مات die 1h2
مارس practice, exercise 3s
مثّل act, perform; represent 2s
محى erase 1d1
مدّ extend; stretch *(tr.)* 1g1
مدح praise (someone) 1s1
مرّ pass (by); stop by 1g2
مرق pass (by); stop by 1s2
مزح joke; kid 1s1
مسح wipe, mop 1s1
مسك hold 1s2 **T-82**
مشّط comb 2s
مِشي walk, go 1d4 **T-83**
مضى sign 1d1
مضّى spend (time) 2d
ملك own 1s2
منع forbid 1s1
موّل finance 2s
ميّز distinguish 2s
نادى call 3d
ناقش discuss 3s
ناك fuck 1h1
نام sleep 1h3 **T-84**
نْبسط have fun, enjoy oneself 7s **T-85**
نبّه warn 2s
نتج produce 1s2
نْتخب elect 8s
نْتزع go bad, spoil *(intr.)*, become ruined 7s
نْتظر wait 8s
نْتقد criticize 8s
نْتهى end *(intr.)* 8d
نجح succeed 1s1
نْحرق burn *(intr.)*; become burned 7s
ندِم regret 1s5
نْرفز get annoyed 11s
نزع spoil, ruin *(tr.)* 1s1
نزف bleed 1s2
نزّل download; make lower; drop off 2s
نزِل go down; descend 1s5
نسخ copy 1s1
نِسي forget 1d3 **T-86**
نشر publish; saw (wood) 1s2
نْشغل become busy 7s
نشِف dry *(intr.)* 1s5
نشّف dry *(tr.)* 2s
نصح advise 1s1
نصِح put on weight; get fat 1s5
نضّف clean 2s
نْضمّ join 7g **T-87**
نطّ jump 1g2
نطر wait 1s3 **T-88**
نْطرد get fired 7s
نطق pronounce 1s2
نظّم organize 2s
نفّ blow one's nose 1g1
نْفجر explode *(intr.)*; erupt 7s
نقّ complain; nag (someone) 1g1
نْقال be said 7h **T-89**
نْقبض get arrested 7s
نفّذ carry out, perform 2s
نقل move (houses); copy; cheat (in class) 1s2
نقّى pick, choose, select 2d
نْكسر break *(intr.)* 7s
نْلغى be canceled 7d **T-90**
نمّل be numb, tingle 2s
نْهار collapse 7h
نهى end, finish 1d1
نَوى intend 1d1
هاجم assault, attack 3s
هبّ blow 1g1
هبط land 1s2
هْتمّ be interested (in بِـ), care (about بِـ) 8g **T-91**
هجر abandon, desert 1s3

هجم attack 1s2
هدّ demolish, break down 1g1
هدى give as a gift 1d1
هرب escape 1s3
هرّب smuggle 2s
هرْول jog, go jogging 11s
هزّ shake 1g1
هلك become exhausted 1s2
هِلِك get tired (exhausted) 1s5
همّ worry, trouble *(tr.)* 1g1
واجه face 3s
وافق approve of 3s
وثِق trust 1s8
وجِع hurt *(intr.)* 1s8
وجّع hurt *(tr.)* 2s
ودّع bid farewell 2s
وسّع widen 2s
وَشْوش whisper 11s
وصف describe 1s3
وُصِل arrive 1s9 **T-92**
وصّل deliver 2s
وظّف employ 2s
وَعد promise 1s4 **T-93**
وَعظ preach 1s4
وعّى wake (up), rouse 2d
وِعي wake up *(intr.)* 1d3
وفّر provide; supply 2s
وقّع drop; sign 2s
وِقِع fall 1s8**T-94**
وقِف stand 1s8 **T-95**
وقّف stop *(tr.)* 2s
وَقّف stop *(tr./intr.)* 2s **T-96**
وِلِد be born 1s8 **T-97**
ولّد give birth 2s
ولّع light (cigarette) 2s

English – Arabic Index

abandon هجر 1s3
abduct خطف 1s3
able to: be ~ قِدِر 1s5 **T-73**; كان فِيو **T-103**
ablution: perform ~ تْوضّى 5d
accept قِبِل 1s5
accompany رافق 3s
accomplish خلّص 2s
accuse تهم 1s2
accustomed: become ~ to تْعوّد 5s
achieve حقّق 2s
acquainted: be ~ with تْعرّف 5s
acquire كسب 1s1
act مثّل 2s
add ضاف 1h1; زاد 1h1; add up جمع 1s1
adjust زبّط 2s
admit (to) فوّت 2s; عْترف 8s
adopt تْبنّى 5d
advise نصح 1s1
affect أثّر 2s
afflict صاب 1h1
afraid: be ~ of خاف 1h3
age ختْير 11s; عجّز 2s
agree قِبِل 1s5; agree (with) (مع) تّفق 8s
allow سمح 1s1; خلّى 2d **T-30**
am → **be**
anger زعّل 2s
angry: become ~ عصّب 2s; زِعِل 1s5
announce أعْلن 4s **T-3**
annoy ضايق 3s
annoyed: become ~ نرْفز 11s
answer جاوب 3s; ردّ على 1g1
anxious: be ~ قِلِق 1s5
apologize (to... for) (لـ ... على) عْتذر 8s
appeal to عجب 1s2
appear ظهر 1s1
applaud زقّف 2s
apply (to) (على) قدّم 2s
appoint عيّن 2s
appreciate قدّر 2s
approve of وافق 3s
are → **be**
argue (with each other) تْخانق 6s; argue with خانق 3s; argue (about) (على) جادل 3s
arrange رتّب 2s
arrest عْتقل 8s; قبض على 1s3
arrested: get ~ نْقبض 7s
arrive وُصِل 1s9 **T-92**
ascend طِلِع 1s5 **T-58**
ask سأل 1s1 **T-42**
assault هاجم 3s; عْتدى 8d
assist ساعد 3s **T-41**
assume فرض 1s3
assure أكّد 2s
attack عْتدى على 8d
attack هجم 1s2; هاجم 3s
attempt حاوَل 3s **T-19**
attend حِضِر 1s5 **T-24**
attract جذب 1s2; شدّ 1g1
avoid تْفادى 6d **T-14**; تْجنّب 5s
bad: go ~ (spoil) نْتزع 7s;
bake خبز 1s2
bandage عصّب 2s
baptize عمّد 2s
bargain ساوم 3s
bark عوّى 2d
bath: take a ~ تْحمّم 5s
be كان 1h2 **T-76**
bear تْحمّل 5s
beat غلب 1s2; ضرب 1s2; دقّ 1g1
become بِقِي 1d3 **T-8**; صار 1h1 **T-53**
beg (for money) شحد 1s1

beg ترجّى 5d
begin بلّش 2s **T-9**
behave تأدّب 5s; تصرّف 5s
belch تدشّى 5d
believe صدّق 2s; believe in آمن بِـ 3s
belong خصّ 1g2
bet راهن 3s
betray خان 1h2
better: get ~ تحسّن 5s; صحّ 1g2; make ~ حسّن 2s
bid farewell ودّع 2s
big: become ~ كبر 1s1
bind ربط 1s3 **T-35**
bite عضّ 1g3
lack: become ~ سْودّ 9s
lacken سوّد 2s
lame لام 1h2
leed نزف 1s2
less بارك 3s; (of God) رزق 1s2
lind: go ~ عمى 1d2
link رفّ 1g1
lock سدّ 1g1
low هبّ 1g1; blow one's nose نفّ 1g1
ue: turn ~ زْرقّ 9s
ush حْمرّ 9s **T-27**
oard (flight etc) طِلِع 1s5 **T-58**
oil (food) سلق 1s2; (water) غلى 1d1
ook حجز 1s2
re (make feel bored) زهّق 2s
red: become ~ زِهِق 1s5
rn: be ~ وِلِد 1s8 **T-97**; خِلِق 1s5
rrow (money) تْديّن 5s; (something) سْتعار 8h
ther ضايق 3s
unce طجّ 1g2
ak *(tr.)* كسر 1s2; *(intr.)* نْكسر 7s; **break** a bill) صرّف 2s; break down هدّ 1g1
akfast: have ~ تْروّق 5s

breastfeed رضّع 2s; be breastfed رِضِع 1s5
breathe تْنفّس 5s
bribe برْطل 11s; رشى 1d1
bring جاب 1h1 **T-18**; bring back ردّ 1g1; bring together ضمّ 1g2
bruise *(intr.)* زْرقّ 9s
brush فرْشى 11d
buckle بكّل 2s
build بنى 1d1; عمّر 2s
burn *(tr.)* حرق 1s2; (food) شاط 1h2; *(intr.)* نْحرق 7s
burp تْدشّى 5d
bury دفن 1s2
busy: become ~ نْشغل 7s
button بكّل 2s
buy شْترى 8d **T-49**
calculate حسب 1s2
call (out) نادى 3d; call to prayer أذّن 2s; (name) سمّى 2d; be called تْسمّى 5d; **call** (phone) تلْفن 11s **T-16**
calm down راق 1h2
can قِدِر 1s5 **T-73**; كان فِيو **T-103**
cancel لغى 1d1; be canceled نْلغى 7d **T-90**
care (about) هْتمّ (بِـ) 8g **T-91**
carry حِمِل 1s6; شال 1h1; carry out (perform) نفّذ 2s; أدّى 2d
catch لقط 1s1; catch up with (someone) لحّق 2s
cause سبّب 2s; خلّى 2d **T-30**
celebrate حْتفل 8s **T-21**
change *(tr.)* غيّر 2s **T-64**; (money) صرّف 2s, صرف 1s2; *(intr.)* تْغيّر 5s; (turn into) تْحوّل 5s; make change (break a bill) صرّف 2s
chase لاحق 3s; لِحِق 1s5
cheat (deceive) غشّ 1g1; (in school) نقل 1s2
check راجع 3s; أكّد 2s; حقّق 2s

cheer شجّع 2s
chew علك 1s2
choke *(intr.)* خْتنق 8s; choke (on food/object) تْشرْدق (بِ) 5s
choose نقّى 8h; خْتار 2d
chop (up) خرّط 2s; فرم 1s2
claim دّعى 8d
clean نضّف 2s
clear: become ~ برز 1s2
click (on) فقس (على) 1s1
cling لزّق 2s
close *(tr.)* سكّر 2s **T-45**; (door) غلق 1s2; (eyes) غمّد 2s; *(intr.)* تْسكّر 5s; (of eyes) غمد 1s3
cold: become ~ برد 1s2
collapse نْهار 7h
collect لمّ 1g1; ضبّ 1g2; جمّع 2s
color لوّن 2s
comb مشّط 2s
come إجا *(irr.)* **T-1**; come back رِجِع 1s5 **T-37**
command أمر 1s3 **T-5**
commit (a crime) رْتكِب 8s
compare قارن 2s
complain نقّ 1g1; شكى 1d1
complete خلّص 2s
comply with لْتزم 8s
compose (music) ألّف 2s; be composed of (made up of) تْكوّن 5s
concern خصّ 1g2
conclude ختم 1s2
condemn دان 1h1
confess عْترف 8s
confirm أكّد 2s
confuse لخْبط 11s; be confused تْلخْبط 12s **T-15**
conjugate (verb) صرّف 2s
connect تّصل مع/بِ 8s
consider عْتبر 8s; consider strange سْتغْرب 10s
consult سْتشار 10h
contact تّصل مع/بِ 8s
contain حْتوى 8d
continue كمّل 2s
control سَيْطر 11s; ظبط 1s3
convict دان 1h1
convince قنع 1s1
cook طبخ 1s3 **T-56**
copy نسخ 1s1; نقل 1s2
correct *(tr.)* صحّح 2s; صلّح 2s; be correct صحّ 1g2
cost *(intr.)* كلّف 2s
cough قحّ 1g2; سعل 1s2
count عدّ 1g1
cover غطّى 2d
crash خبط 1s3
crawl حبى 1d1
create كوّن 2s; خلق 1s2
criticize نْتقد 8s
cross قِطِع 1s5; cross out شطب 1s3
cry بِكي 1d4
cure عالج 3s; صحّ 1g2
curse سبّ 1g1
cut قطش 1s3; قصّ 1g2; قطّع 2s
damage دمّر 2s
dampen بلّ 1g1
dance رقص 1s2
dark: become ~ سْودّ 9s
darn (socks, etc.) رقّع 2s
deal with تْعامل مع 6s **T-11**
decay *(intr.)* عفّن 2s
deceive خدع 1s1; ضحك على 1s5 **T-54**
decide قرّر 2s
declare أعْلن 4s **T-3**; صرّح 2s
decline (word) صرّف 2s
decrease *(tr.)* قلّل 2s; قلّ 1g1
defeat غلب 1s2

defend دافع 3s
define حدّد 2s
delay *(tr.)* أخّر 2s; be delayed تْأجّل 5s
deliver سلّم 2s; وصّل 2s
demolish هدّ 1g1
demonstrate بيّن 2s; تْظاهر 6s
deny أنْكر 4s
depart فلّ 1g1
depend on عْتمد على 8s
deposit (in bank) حطّ 1g3 **T-25**
deprive حرم 1s2
descend نِزِل 1s5
describe وصف 1s3
desert هجر 1s3
deserve سْتاهل 10 *(irr.)*
design صمّم 2s
develop *(intr.)* تْطوّر 5s
diagnose شخّص 2s
die مات 1h2
differ from خْتلف مع/مِن 8s
dig بحش 1s1; حفر 1s3
dinner: have ~ تْعشّى 5d
disagree (with) خْتلف (مع) 8s
disappear خْتفى 8d
discipline أدّب 2s
discover كْتشف 8s
discuss ناقش 3s
dismiss (from a job) صرف 1s2
display بسط 1s3
dissolve *(tr.)* دوّب 2s; *(intr.)* داب 1h2
distinguish ميّز 2s
disturb ضايق 3s
dive غاص 1h2; غطس 1s3
divide قسم 1s2
divorce طلّق 2s; get divorced تْطلّق 5s
do عِمِل 1s7 **T-62**; ساوى 3d; do without سْتغنى 10d
dodge تْفادى 6d **T-14**
doing: be ~ قعد 1s2 **T-75**
doubt شكّ 1g1
download نزّل 2s; داوْنْلود، يْداوْنْلِد *(irr.)* foreign)
doze off طبّ 1g2
drag جرّ 1g1; شدّ 1g1
draw رسم 1s2
dream حِلِم 1s5
drink شرب 1s5 **T-51**
drive ساق 1h2
drop وقّع 2s; drop off نزّل 2s
drunk: get ~ سِكِر 1s5
dry *(tr.)* نشّف 2s; *(intr.)* نِشِف 1s5
dye (one's hair) صبغ 1s2
earn قبض 1s1 **T-71**
eat أكل *(irr.)* **T-4**
edit صلّح 2s
elect نْتخب 8s
embrace ضمّ 1g2
embroider طرّز 2s
employ وظّف 2s; شغّل 2s
employment: obtain ~ تْوظّف 5s
empty فضّى 2d
empty: become ~ فِضي 1d3
encourage شجّع 2s
end *(tr.)* نهى 1d1; خلّص 2s; *(intr.)* نْتهى 8d; خِلِص 1s5 **T-28**
endure تْحمّل 5s
enjoy سْتمْتع 10s; سْتهنّى بـ 10 *(irr.)* **T-44**; enjoy oneself تْسلّى 5d, نْبسط 7s **T-85**
enlarge كبّر 2s
enlist جنّد 2s
enroll تْسجّل 5s
enter فات 1h2
entertain سلّى 2d
equal ساوى 3d
erase محى 1d1
err تْلخْبط 12s **T-15**
erupt نْفجر 7s; ثار 1h2
escape فلت 1s2; هرب 1s3

establish أسّس 2s; ثبّت 2s
estimate قدّر 2s
examine فحص 1s1
excuse عذر 1s2
exercise مارس 3s; تْمرّن 5s
exhaust هلك 1s2; become exhausted هِلِك 1s5
expect تْوقّع 5s
expensive: become ~ غِلي 1d3
explain شرح 1s1; فسّر 2s
explode *(intr.)* نْفجر 7s
explore سْتكشف 10s
express عبّر عن 2s
extend مدّ 1g1
extinguish طفّى 2d
face واجه 3s
fail سقط 1s2
fall وِقِع 1s8 **T-94**; fall asleep غِفي 1d3
far: become ~ بِعِد 1s6
farewell: bid ~ ودّع 2s
fart ضرّط 2s
fast صام 1h2
fasten بكّل 2s; ثبّت 2s; ربط 1s3 **T-35**
fat: get ~ نِصِح 1s5; طِخِن 1s5
fear خاف مِن 1h3
feel حسّ بِـ 1g1 **T-23**; شعر بِـ 1s2
fence in سيّج 2s
fight with خانق 3s; قتل 1s2 **T-**72; fight with each other تْخانق 6s;
file (down) برد 1s2
fill عبّى 2d; حشى 1d1; fill in/out (a form) عبّى 2d
finance موّل 2s
find لاقى 3d **T-79**
finish *(tr.)* خلّص 2s **T-29**; نهى 1d1; ختم 1s2; *(intr.)* خِلِص 1s5 **T-28**
fire طرد 1s2; صرف 1s2; get fired نْطرد 7s
fish صْطاد 8h
fit *(tr.)* ظبط 1s3
fix صلّح 2s; حدّد 2s; fix (in place) ثبّت 2s
float طاف 1h2; فاش 1h2
flood طاف 1h2
fly طار 1h1
fold طوى 1d1
follow لِحِق 1s5; follow (a recipe, etc.) تبع 1s1
forbid منع 1s1; (in religion) حرّم 2s
force (someone to do) جبر 1s2
forget نِسي 1d3 **T-86**
forgive غفر 1s2; سامح 3s
form شكّل 2s; كوّن 2s
found (establish) أسّس 2s
freeze *(intr.)* تْجمّد 5s
frighten خوّف 2s
frown عبس 1s2; كشّر 2s
fry *(tr.)* قلى 1d1
fuck ناك 1h1
full: become ~ (of food) شِبِع 1s5
fun: have ~ نْبسط 7s **T-85**; تْسلّى 5d
gain كسب 1s1; رِبِح 1s5
gather لمّ 1g1; ضبّ 1g2; جمّع 2s
gaze بحْلق 11s
get جاب 1h1 **T-18**; حاز على 1h2; get along with تّفق مع 8s; get away فلت 1s2; get rid of تْخلّص مِن 5s; get up فاق 1h1 **T-65**, قام 1h2
give عطى 1d *(irr.)* **T-61**; (as a gift) هدى 1d1; give back رجّع 2s; give a ride to ركّب 2s; give an order أمر 1s3 **T-5**; give birth ولّد 2s
go راح 1h2 **T-34**; مِشي 1d4 **T-83**; go back رِجِع 1s5 **T-37**; go down نِزِل 1s5; go out ضهر 1s1; go up طِلِع 1s5 **T-58**
govern حكم 1s2
graduate (from) تْخرّج (مِن) 5s
grate برش 1s2
graze رعى 1d2
green: turn ~ خْضرّ 9s

reet سْتقبْل 10s; سلّم على 2s
rind طحن 1s1
row (a plant) زرع 1s1; grow (up) كبر 1s1; grow old عجّز 2s
uard حرس 1s2
uess حِزِر 1s5
uide دلّ 1g1
aggle over ساوم 3s
ammer دقّ 1g1
ang *(tr.)* علّق 2s; hang out (with friends) كزْدر 11s
appen صار 1h1 **T-53**
arvest حصد 1s3; جمع 1s1
ate كِرِه 1s5
ave كان عِنْدو **T-99**; كان إلو **T-100**; كان معو **T-101**
ead toward تْوجّه لـ 5s
eal صحّ 1g2
ear سمع 1s5 **T-47**
eat (up) *(tr.)* سخّن 2s
elp ساعد 3s **T-41**
esitate تْردّد 5s
ide خبّى 2d
igh: make ~ علّى 2d
ire شغّل 2s
it ضرب 1s2; سفق 1s2; (a target) صاب 1h1
old مسك 1s2 **T-82**
ope تْمنّى 5d **T-17**
ug عبط 1s3
umiliate (cause to lose face) بخع 1s1
ungry: become ~ جاع 1h2
unt صْطاد 8h
urt *(tr.)* جرح 1s1, وجّع 2s; *(intr.)* وِجِع 1s8
nagine تْخيّل 5s; تْصوّر 5s
npose (on) فرض (على) 1s3
nprison حبس 1s2
nprove *(tr.)* حسّن 2s; *(intr.)* تْحسّن 5s
clude شمل 1s2
crease *(tr.)* كتّر 2s; *(intr.)* زاد 1h1

indicate دلّ 1g1
inflect (word) صرّف 2s
influence أثّر 2s
inform بلّغ 2s; خبّر 2s
initiate بادر 3s
injure جرح 1s1
insist لحّ 1g1
instruct أمر 1s3 **T-5**
intend نَوى 1d1
interested: be ~ (in) هْتمّ (بـِ) 8g **T-91**
interrogate سْتجْوب 10s
interrupt قطش 1s3
interview قابل 3s
introduce (someone to) عرّف (على) 2s
invite عزم 1s2 **T-60**
iron كوى 1d1
irrigate صقى 1d1
is → be
issue صدر 1s3
itch حكّ 1g1
jog هرْول 11s
join شْترك 8s; نْضمّ 7g **T-87**
joke مزح 1s1
jump فزّ 1g1; نطّ 1g2
keep خلّى 2d **T-30**; keep doing (continue to do) ضلّ 1g3 **T-55**
kick زعب 1s1; لبط 1s3; (a ball) شاط 1h2
kid مزح 1s1
kidnap خطف 1s3
kill قتل 1s2 **T-72**
kiss باس 1h2
knit: ~ one's brow عبس 1s2
knock دقّ 1g1
know عِرِف 1s7 **T-59**
land هبط 1s2
late: be ~ تْأخّر 5s
laugh ضحك 1s5 **T-54**; make laugh ضحّك 2s
lay حطّ 1g3 **T-25**; lay (an egg) باض 1h1

lead قاد 1h2
learn تْعلّم 5s **T-12**
leave فلّ 1g1; ضهر 1s1; ترك 1s2 **T-10**
lend عار 1h2; (money) ديّن 2s
lessen خفّف 2s
let خلّى 2d **T-30**; let in فوّت 2s
liberate حرّر 2s
lick لحس 1s1
lie كذّب 2s **T-78**; lie to (deceive) ضحك 1s5 **T-54**
lift شال 1h1; lift and carry شقل 1s2
light (a cigarette) ولّع 2s
lighten خفّف 2s
like حبّ 1g1 **T-20**
link ربط 1s3 **T-35**
listen (to) سمع 1s5 **T-47**
live عاش 1h2; سكن 1s2 **T-46**; live without سْتغنى 10d
lock قفّل 2s
long for شْتاق 8h
look (at) تْطلّع (في/بـ) 5s; شاف 1h2 **T-48**; look for دوّر 2s; look like شِبِه 1s5
lose ضيّع 2s; lose (game) خِسِر 1s5; lose weight ضِعِف 1s5
lost: get ~ ضاع 1h1
love حبّ 1g1 **T-20**; love passionately عِشِق 1s5
lower نزّل 2s
lunch: have ~ تْغدّى 5d **T-13**
mail بعت 1s1
maintain حافظ على 3s
major (in) تْخصّص (بـ) 5s
make عِمِل 1s7 **T-62**; (force, cause) خلّى 2d **T-30**
manage (to do) لحّق 2s
manufacture صنع 1s1
married: get ~ to تْجوّز 5s
massage دلّك 2s
mean قصد 1s3
measure قاس 1h1
meet تْعرّف 5s; (with) جْتمع (مع) 8s; meet up with لْتقى بـ 8d
melt *(tr.)* دوّب 2s; *(intr.)* داب 1h2
memorize حِفِظ 1s5
mention ذكر 1s2
milk حلب 1s2
mince فرم 1s2
miss شْتاق 8h
mistake: make a ~ تْلخْبط 12s **T-15**
mix up لخْبط 11s
mix خلط 1s3; become mixed up تْلخْبط 12s **T-15**
mop مسح 1s1
mourn حِزِن 1s5
move *(tr.)* حرّك 2s **T-22**; *(intr.)* تْحرّك 5s; move (houses) نقل 1s2; move (something) out of the way زاح 1h1
multiply ضرب 1s2
nag (someone) نقّ 1g1
name سمّى 2d
named: be ~ تْسمّى 5d
nap تْصطّح 5s
need حْتاج 8s; عاز 1h2
nominate رشّح 2s
notice لاحظ 3s
numb: be ~ نمّل 2s
observe لْتزم 8s
obtain حاز على 1h2; حصل على 1s1
occupy حْتلّ 8g
off work: be ~ قعد 1s2 **T-75**
offer عرض 1s3; قدّم 2s
old: become ~ ختْير 11s
open فتح 1s1 **T-66**
operate شغّل 2s
oppose عاكس 3s
optimistic: be ~ تْفاءل 6s
order طلب 1s2 **T-57**
organize نظّم 2s

vertake دوْبل 11s; تْجاوز 6s
wn ملك 1s2
ack (a suitcase) ضبّ 1g2
aint دهن 1s1
ale: become ~ بْيضّ 9s
alpitate دقّ 1g1
ark (car) صفّ 1g2
articipate in بِ شْترك 8s
ass دوْبل 11s; تْجاوز 6s; قِطِع 1s5; pass (by) مرق 1s2, فات 1h2, مرّ 1g2; pass away تْوفّى 5d
atch رقّع 2s
ay off (debt) سدّد 2s
ay دفع 1s1 **T-32**
ee شخّ 1g2; بوّل 2s
eep بصْبص 11s
erform أدّى 2d; نقّد 2s; (act) مثّل 2s; perform ritual ablutions تْوضّى 5d
ermit سمح 1s1
essimistic: be ~ تْشاءم 6s
hone تلْفن 11s **T-16**
hotocopy صوّر 2s
hotograph صوّر 2s; have one's ~ taken تْصوّر 5s; be photographed تْصوّر 5s
ick نقّى 2d; ~ up ركّب 2s, شال 1h1
icture: have one's ~ taken تْصوّر 5s
iss شخّ 1g2
ity شِفِق على 1s5
lace حطّ 1g3 **T-25**
lan خطّط 2s
lant (a seed) زرع 1s1
lay لِعِب 1s5 **T-81**; (instrument) عزف 1s2
lead تْرجّى 5d
lease عجب 1s2; be pleased رِضي 1d3
low حرث 1s2; فلح 1s1
oint (to) (على) دلّ 1g1
olish فرك 1s2
ostpone أجّل 2s
our صبّ 1g2; دلق 1s2

practice مارس 3s; تْدرّب على 5s; تْمرّن 5s
praise مدح 1s1
pray دعا 1d1; (ritual prayer) صلّى 2d
preach وَعظ 1s4; (بِـ) بشّر 2s
prefer فضّل 2s
pregnant: get ~ حِبِل 1s5
prepare جهّز 2s; حضّر 2s; (food) طبخ 1s3 **T-56**
present قدّم 2s; عرض 1s3
pressure لحّ 1g1
print طبع 1s1
produce نتج 1s2
promise وَعد 1s4 **T-93**
promoted: be ~ (at work) تْرقّى 5d
pronounce نطق 1s2
propose قرض 1s3
protect حمى 1d4
protest حْتجّ 8g; تْظاهر 6s
prove برْهن 11s
provide وفّر 2s
publish نشر 1s2; أصْدر 4s
pull شدّ 1g1; جرّ 1g1
puncture بخْوش 11s
punish جازى 3d
pursue لاحق 3s
push دفش 1s2
put حطّ 1g3 **T-25**; put aside (money) صمّد 2s; put away ضبّ 1g2; put in فوّت 2s; put on weight نِصِح 1s5
qualify أهّل 2s
quarrel *(intr.)* تْخانق 6s
quiet: be ~ خِرِس 1s5; سكت 1s2
quit بطّل 2s; ترك 1s2 **T-10**
rain شتّى 2d
raise رفع 1s1
rape غْتصب 8s
reach طال 1h3
read قرا 1d2 **T-74**
ready: get ~ سْتعدّ 10g

realize حقّق 2s
receive سْتلم 8s
reciprocate بادل 3s
record سجّل 2s
recover صحّ 1g2
recruit جنّد 2s
red: turn ~ حْمرّ 9s **T-27**
reduce *(tr.)* قلّل 2s; reduce *(intr.)* قلّ 1g1
refuse رفض 1s3
regret نِدِم 1s5; تْأسّف 5s
relax رخّى 2d; رْتاح 8h **T-36**
religious: become ~ تْديّن 5s
remain بِقي 1d3 **T-8**; (in a place) ضلّ 1g3 **T-55**
remember تْذكّر 5s فاق 1h2
remind ذكّر 2s; فوّق 2s
remove شال 1h1; فكّ 1g1; (clothes) شلح 1s1
renew جدّد 2s
rent (from) (مِن) سْتأجر 10s; rent (to) (لـ) أجّر 2s
repair صلّح 2s
repeat عاد 1h1
repent تاب 1h2
replace بدّل 2s
reply ردّ 1g1; جاوب 3s
report بلّغ 2s
represent رمز 1s2; مثّل 2s
request طلب 1s2 **T-57**
require عاز 1h2
resemble شِبِه 1s5
resent حقد 1s3
reserve حجز 1s2
resign سْتقال 10h
respect حْترم 8s
respond to جاوب 3s
rest رْتاح 8h **T-36**
retire تْقاعد 6s
return *(tr.)* رجّع 2s; ردّ 1g1; *(intr.)* رِجِع 1s5 **T-37**
reveal بيّن 2s
review راجع 3s
revise راجع 3s
rid: get ~ of تْخلّص مِن 5s
ride رِكِب 1s5 **T-38**
ring رنّ 1g1; (doorbell) دقّ 1g1
rinse شطف 1s2
rise قام 1h2; (of sun) شرق 1s2
roam (around) برم 1s2 **T-7**; دار 1h2
rot عفّن 2s
rouse وعّى 2d
rub فرك 1s2; حفّ 1g1
ruin *(tr.)* نزع 1s1; become ruined نْتزع 7s
run ركض 1s2; (flow) جرى 1d1
said: be ~ نْقال 7h **T-89**
save صمّد 2s; (computer) حِفِظ 1s5, سايْف، يْسايِف *(irr.)* (foreign)
saw (wood) نشر 1s2
say قال 1h2 **T-70**
scare خوّف 2s
scowl عبس 1s2
scrape حكّ 1g1
scratch حكّ 1g1; جلف 1s2
scream عيّط 2s
seal سدّ 1g1
search (for) (على) دوّر 2s
see شاف 1h2 **T-48**
select نقّى 2d
sell باع 1h1 **T-6**
send بعت 1s1
sense حسّ 1g1 **T-23**
separate فصل 1s3
serve خدم 1s2
set حدّد 2s
settle سدّد 2s
sew خيّط 2s
shake خضّ 1g2; هزّ 1g1

arpen (a pencil) برى 1d1
ave حلق 1s2
ear (a sheep) جزّ 1g1
ine لمع 1s1
ock خضّ 1g2
oot (goal) شاط 1h2
out عيّط 2s
ove دفش 1s2
ow (to) فرْجى (على) 11d **T-67**; بيّن 2s; show (the way) دلّ 1g1
ut *(tr.)* سكّر 2s **T-45**; shut up (be quiet) سكت 1s2
gn مضى 1d1; وقّع 2s
lent: keep ~ خِرِس 1s5
ng غنّى 2d
nk غِرِق 1s5
t قعد 1s2 **T-75**
i تْزلّج 5s
am سفق 1s2
eep نام 1h3 **T-84**
ip زحط 1s1
ow down *(tr.)* خفّف 2s
nell *(tr.)* شمّ 1g1
nile بْتسم 8s
noke دخّن 2s; شرب 1s5 **T-51**
nuggle هرّب 2s
atch خلع 1s1
eeze عطس 1s3
ore شخّر 2s
lve حلّ 1g1
rry: be ~ تْأسّف 5s
rt (in rows) صفّ 1g2
eak حِكي 1d4 **T-26**; speak harshly زعب 1s1
ecialize (in) تْخصّص (بـِ) 5s
eed تْخطّى 5d
end (money) صرف 1s2; (time) مضّى 2d
ill كبّ 1g1
it بزق 1s2

spoil *(tr.)* نزع 1s1; *(intr.)* نْتزع 7s
spray بخّ 1g1
spread out بسط 1s3
stamp ختم 1s2
stand وِقِف 1s8 **T-95**
staple كبس 1s2
stare بحْلق 11s
start بلّش 2s **T-9**; start to (do) صار 1h1 **T-53**
state صرّح 2s
stay بِقي 1d3 **T-8**; ضلّ 1g3 **T-55**; قعد 1s2 **T-75**; stay up late سِهِر 1s5
steal سرق 1s2
step دعس 1s1
stick لزّق 2s
stingy: become ~ بِخِل 1s5
stitches: get ~ تْقطّب 5s
stop *(tr./intr.)* وَقّف 2s **T-96**; *(intr.)* خِلِص 1s5 **T-28;** stop by مرق 1s2, مرّ 1g2
strange: consider ~ سْتغْرب 10s
stretch *(tr.)* مدّ 1g1
strike سفق 1s2
study درس 1s2 **T-31**; تْعلّم 5s **T-12**
stuff حشى 1d1
submerge غاص 1h2; غطس 1s3
submit قدّم 2s
subtract طرح 1s1
succeed نجح 1s1
suckle رِضِع 1s5
suffer عانى 3d
suffocate خْتنق 8s
suggest قرض 1s3; قْترح 8s
supply وفّر 2s
support سند 1s2
suppose فرض 1s3; فْترض 8s
surprise فاجئ 3s
surprised: be ~ تْفاجئ 6s
swallow بلع 1s1; swallow the wrong way تْشرْدق 5s

swear سبّ 1g1; swear (by) حلف 1s2
sweat عِرِق 1s5
sweep كنّس 2s
swim سبح 1s1
switch: ~ off طفّى 2d; ~ on ضوّى 2d
symbolize رمز 1s2
take أخد *(irr.)* **T-2**; **take away** شال 1h1; take off (clothes) شلح 1s1; take out طلّع 2s; take up(stairs) طلّع 2s
talk حِكي 1d4 **T-26**; حاكى 3d
tan سْمرّ 9s
taste داق 1h2
teach درّس 2s; علّم 2s
tear خزّق 2s
telephone تلْفن 11s **T-16**
tell (to) خبرّ 2s; قال (لـ) 1h2 **T-70**; (a story) حِكي 1d4 **T-26**
terminate (fire) خلّص 2s **T-29**
thank شكر 1s2 **T-52**
thaw *(tr.)* دوّب 2s; *(intr.)* داب 1h2
think (about) فكّر (في) 2s **T-68**; (believe) عْتقد 8s; **think** (be of the opinion) فْتكر 8s
thirsty: become ~ عِطِش 1s5
throw زتّ 1g1; رمى 1d1 **T-39**; throw away زتّ 1g1; throw up تْفوّع 5s
tidy up ضبّ 1g2
tie ربط 1s3 **T-35**
tighten شدّ 1g1
tingle نمّل 2s
tip (give a gratuity) بخْشش 11s
tired: become ~ تِعِب 1s5; هِلِك 1s5
tolerate تْحمّل 5s
torture عذّب 2s
touch دقر 1s1 **T-33**; لمس 1s2
train أهّل 2s; درّب 2s
translate ترْجم 11s; be translated تْرجْم 12s
travel سافر 3s
tread (on) دعس (على) 1s1
treat عالج 3s; تْعامل مع 6s **T-11**
trim (beard) زبّط 2s
trip *(tr.)* فرْكش 11s; *(intr.)* تْفرْكش 12s
trouble *(tr.)* همّ 1g1
trust وِثِق 1s8
try حاوَل 3s **T-19**; try (out) جرّب 2s
tune (instrument) لحّن 2s
turn *(tr.)* لفّ 1g1; **turn (around)** برم 1s2 **T-7**; *(intr.)* فرق 1s3; (tr/intr.) دار 1h2; turn into تْحوّل 5s; turn off طفّى 2d; turn on ضوّى 2d; turn up (volume) علّى 2d
unbutton فكّ 1g1
understand فِهِم 1s5 **T-69**; understand each other تْفاهم 6s
undo فكّ 1g1
undress *(tr.)* شلّح 2s; *(intr.)* شلح 1s1
unpack فضّى 2d
untie فكّ 1g1
upset *(tr.)* زعّل 2s; become ~ زِعِل 1s5
urinate شخّ 1g2; بوّل 2s
use سْتعْمل 10s **T-43**; سْتخْدم 10s
used: get ~ to تْعوّد 5s
useful: be ~ فاد 1h1
vacate فضّى 2d
value قدّر 2s
vandalize خرّب 2s
verify حقّق 2s; أكّد 2s
visit زار 1h2 **T-40**; برم 1s2 **T-7**
vomit تْفوّع 5s
vote صوّت 2s
wait نطر 1s3 **T-88**; نْتظر 8s; سْتنّى 10d
wake (up) *(tr.)* فيّق 2s, وعّى 2d; *(intr.)* فاق 1h1 **T-65**, وِعي 1d3
walk مِشي 1d4 **T-83**; go for a ~ تْمشّى 5d
want حبّ 1g1 **T-20**
warn نبّه 2s
was → **be**

ash غسّل 2s **T-63**; wash (dishes) جلى 1d1
atch حِضِر 1s5 **T-24**; تْفرّج على 5s
ater (a plant) سقى 1d1
ear لِبس 1s6 **T-80**; wear a hijab تْحجّب 5s
eigh زان 1h1
eight: lose ~ ضِعِف 1s5
elcome أهّل 2s; سْتقْبل 10s
ere → be
et بلّ 1g1
hisper وَشْوش 11s
hite: become ~ بْيضّ 9s
hiten بيّض 2s
iden وسّع 2s
in كسب 1s1; ربِح 1s5; (game) فاز 1h2
ink غمز 1s2
wipe مسح 1s1
wish تْمنّى 5d **T-17**
withdraw سحب 1s1
work (as) شْتغل 8s **T-50**; make work (put to work) شغّل 2s; work hard فلح 1s1; work out (exercise) تْمرّن 5s; work out (successfully) ظبط 1s3; work with (deal with) تْعامل مع 6s **T-11**
worry *(tr.)* همّ 1g1; *(intr.)* قِلِق 1s5
wound جرح 1s1
wrap لفّ 1g1
write كتب 1s2 **T-77**
yawn تّاوب 6s
yell عيّط 2s
yellow: turn ~ صْفرّ 9s

Made in the USA
San Bernardino, CA
03 June 2020

72476804R00093